The Inflexible Captive by Hannah More

Hannah More was born on February 2nd, 1745 at Fishponds in the parish of Stapleton, near Bristol. She was the fourth of five daughters.

The City of Bristol, at that time, was a centre for slave-trading and Hannah would, over time, become one of its staunchest critics.

She was keen to learn, possessed a sharp intellect and was assiduous in studying. Hannah first wrote in 1762 with The Search after Happiness (by the mid-1780s some 10,000 copies had been sold).

In 1767 Hannah became engaged to William Turner. After six years, with no wedding in sight, the engagement was broken off. Turner then bestowed upon her an annual annuity of £200. This was enough to meet her needs and set her free to pursue a literary career.

Her first play, The Inflexible Captive, was staged at Bath in 1775. The famous David Garrick himself produced her next play, Percy, in 1777 as well as writing both the Prologue and Epilogue for it. It was a great success when performed at Covent Garden in December of that year.

Hannah turned to religious writing with Sacred Dramas in 1782; it rapidly ran through nineteen editions. These and the poems Bas-Bleu and Florio (1786) mark her gradual transition to a more serious and considered view of life.

Hannah contributed much to the newly-founded Abolition Society including, in February 1788, her publication of Slavery, a Poem recognised as one of the most important of the abolition period.

Her work now became more evangelical. In the 1790s she wrote several Cheap Repository Tracts which covered moral, religious and political topics and were both for sale or distributed to literate poor people. The most famous is, perhaps, The Shepherd of Salisbury Plain, describing a family of incredible frugality and contentment. Two million copies of these were circulated, in one year.

In 1789, she purchased a small house at Cowslip Green in Somerset. She was instrumental in setting up twelve schools in the area by 1800.

She continued to oppose slavery throughout her life, but at the time of the Abolition Bill of 1807, her health did not permit her to take as active a role in the movement as she had done in the late 1780s, although she maintained a correspondence with Wilberforce and others.

In July 1833, the Bill to abolish slavery throughout the British Empire passed in the House of Commons, followed by the House of Lords on August 1st.

Hannah More died on September 7th, 1833.

Index of Contents

DEDICATION

MY DEAR MADAM,

It seems somewhat extraordinary that although with persons of great merit and delicacy no virtue stands in higher estimation than truth, yet, in such an address as the present, there would be some danger of offending them by a strict adherence to it; I mean by uttering truths so generally acknowledged, that every one, except the person addressed, would acquit the writer of flattery. And it will be a singular circumstance to see a Dedication without praise, to a lady possessed of every quality and accomplishment which can justly entitle her to it.

I am,

MY DEAR MADAM,
With great respect,
your most obedient,
and very obliged humble servant,

THE ARGUMENT

Among the great names which have done honour to antiquity in general, and to the Roman Republic in particular, that of Marcus Attilius Regulus has, by the general consent of all ages, been considered as one of the most splendid, since he not only sacrificed his labours, his liberty, and his life for the good of his country, but by a greatness of soul, almost peculiar to himself, contrived to make his very misfortunes contribute to that glorious end.

After the Romans had met with various successes in the first Punic war, under the command of Regulus, victory at length declared for the opposite party, the Roman army was totally overthrown, and Regulus himself taken prisoner, by Xantippus, a Lacedæmonian General in the service of the Carthaginians: the victorious enemy exulting in so important a conquest, kept him many years in close imprisonment, and loaded him with the most cruel indignities. They thought it was now in their power to make their own terms with Rome, and determined to send Regulus thither with their ambassador, to negotiate a peace, or at least an exchange of captives, thinking he would gladly persuade his countrymen to discontinue a war, which necessarily prolonged his captivity. They previously exacted from him an oath to return should his embassy prove unsuccessful; at the same time giving him to understand, that he must expect to suffer a cruel death if he failed in it; this they artfully intimated as the strongest motive for him to leave no means unattempted to accomplish their purpose.

At the unexpected arrival of this venerable hero, the Romans expressed the wildest transports of joy, and would have submitted to almost any conditions to procure his enlargement; but Regulus, so far from availing himself of his influence with the Senate to obtain any personal advantages, employed it to induce them to reject proposals so evidently tending to dishonour their country, declaring his fixed resolution to return to bondage and death, rather than violate his oath.

He at last extorted from them their consent; and departed amidst the tears of his family, the importunites of his friends, the applauses of the Senate, and the tumultuous opposition of the people; and, as a great poet of his own nation beautifully observes, "he embarked for Carthage as calm and unconcerned as if, on finishing the tedious law-suits of his clients, he was retiring to Venafrian fields, or the sweet country of Tarentum."

This piece is, in many parts, a pretty close imitation of the Attilio Regolo of Metastasio, but enlarged and extended into a tragedy of five acts. Historical truth has in general been followed, except in some less essential instances, particularly that of placing the return of Regulus to Rome posterior to the death of his wife. The writer herself never considered the plot as sufficiently bustling and dramatic for representation.

DRAMATIS PERSONÆ

REGULUS,	Mr. Henderson.
PUBLIUS, his Son,	Mr. Dimond.
MANLIUS, the Consul,	Mr. Blisset.
LICINIUS, a Tribune,	Mr. Brown.
HAMILCAR, the Carthaginian } Ambassador, }	Mr. Rowbotham.

ATTILIA, daughter of Regulus,	Miss Mansell.
BARCE, a Carthaginian captive,	Miss Wheeler.

GUARDS, LICTORS, PEOPLE, &c.

SCENE—Near the Gates of Rome

THE INFLEXIBLE CAPTIVE

PROLOGUE

Deep in the bosom of departed days,
Where the first gems of human glory blaze;
Where, crown'd with flowers, in wreaths immortal drest,
The sacred shades of ancient virtue rest;
With joy they search, who joy can feel, to find
Some honest reason still to love mankind.
There the fair foundress of the scene to-night
Explores the paths that dignify delight;
The regions of the mighty dead pervades;
The Sibyl she that leads us to the shades.
O may each blast of ruder breath forbear
To waft her light leaves on the ruthless air,
Since she, as heedless, strives not to maintain
This tender offspring of her teeming brain!
For this poor birth was no provision made,
A flower that sprung and languish'd in the shade.
On Avon's banks, forsaken and forlorn,
This careless mother left her elder born;
And though unlike what Avon hail'd of yore,
Those giant sons that Shakspeare's banners bore,
Yet may we yield this little offspring grace,
And love the last and least of such a race.
Shall the strong scenes, where senatorial Rome,
Mourn'd o'er the rigour of her patriot's doom;
Where melting Nature aw'd by Virtue's eye,
Hid the big drop, and held the bursting sigh;
Where all that majesty of soul can give,
Truth, Honour, Pity, fair Affection live;
Shall scenes like these, the glory of an age,
Gleam from the press, nor triumph on the stage?
Forbid it, Britons! and, as Romans brave,
Like Romans boast one citizen to save.

ACT I

SCENE—A Hall in the Consul's Palace

Enter LICINIUS, **ATTILIA**, **LICTORS** and **PEOPLE**.

LICINIUS
Attilia waiting here? Is't possible?
Is this a place for Regulus's daughter?
Just gods! must that incomparable maid
Associate here with Lictors and Plebeians?

ATTILIA
Yes, on this threshold patiently I wait
The Consul's coming; I would make him blush
To see me here his suitor. O Licinius,
This is no time for form and cold decorum;
Five lagging years have crept their tedious round,
And Regulus, alas! is still a slave,
A wretched slave, unpitied, and forgotten;
No other tribute paid his memory,
Than the sad tears of his unhappy child;
If she be silent, who will speak for Regulus?

LICINIUS
Let not her sorrows make my fair unjust.
Is there in Rome a heart so dead to virtue
That does not beat in Regulus's cause?
That wearies not the gods for his return?
That does not think all subjugated Afric
A slender, unimportant acquisition,
If, in return for this extended empire,
The freedom of thy father be the purchase?
These are the feelings of Imperial Rome;
My own, it were superfluous to declare.
For if Licinius were to weigh his merit,
That he's thy father were sufficient glory.
He was my leader, train'd me up to arms;
And if I boast a spark of Roman honour,
I owe it to his precepts and his virtues.

ATTILIA
And yet I have not seen Licinius stir.

LICINIUS
Ah! spare me thy reproaches—what, when late
A private citizen, could I attempt?
'Twas not the lust of power, or pride of rank,
Which made me seek the dignity of tribune;
No, my Attilia, but I fondly hop'd
'Twould strengthen and enforce the just request

Which as a private man I vainly urg'd;
But now, the people's representative,
I shall demand, Attilia, to be heard.

ATTILIA
Ah! let us not too hastily apply
This dang'rous remedy; I would not rouse
Fresh tumults 'twixt the people and the senate:
Each views with jealousy the idol, Power,
Which, each possessing, would alike abuse.
What one demands the other still denies.
Might I advise you, try a gentler method;
I know that every moment Rome expects
Th' ambassador of Carthage, nay, 'tis said
The Conscript Fathers are already met
To give him audience in Bellona's temple.
There might the Consul at my suit, Licinius,
Propose the ransom of my captive father.

LICINIUS
Ah! think, Attilia, who that Consul is,
Manlius, thy father's rival, and his foe:
His ancient rival, and his foe profess'd:
To hope in him, my fair, were fond delusion.

ATTILIA
Yet though his rival, Manlius is a Roman:
Nor will he think of private enmities,
Weigh'd in the balance with the good of Rome:
Let me at least make trial of his honour.

LICINIUS
Be it so, my fair! but elsewhere make thy suit;
Let not the Consul meet Attilia here,
Confounded with the refuse of the people.

ATTILIA
Yes, I will see him here, e'en here, Licinius.
Let Manlius blush, not me: here will I speak,
Here shall he answer me.

LICINIUS
Behold he comes.

ATTILIA
Do thou retire.

LICINIUS

O bless me with a look,
One parting look at least.

ATTILIA
Know, my Licinius,
That at this moment I am all the daughter,
The filial feelings now possess my soul,
And other passions find no entrance there.

LICINIUS
O sweet, yet powerful influence of virtue,
That charms though cruel, though unkind subdues,
And what was love exalts to admiration!
Yes, 'tis the privilege of souls like thine
To conquer most when least they aim at conquest.
Yet, ah! vouchsafe to think upon Licinius,
Nor fear to rob thy father of his due;
For surely virtue and the gods approve
Unwearied constancy and spotless love.

[Exit **LICINIUS**.

[Enter **MANLIUS**.

ATTILIA
Ah! Manlius, stay, a moment stay, and hear me.

MANLIUS
I did not think to meet thee here, Attilia;
The place so little worthy of the guest.

ATTILIA
It would, indeed, have ill become Attilia,
While still her father was a Roman citizen;
But for the daughter of a slave to Carthage,
It surely is most fitting.

MANLIUS
Say, Attilia,
What is the purpose of thy coming hither!

ATTILIA
What is the purpose, patience, pitying heaven!
Tell me, how long, to Rome's eternal shame,
To fill with horror all the wond'ring world,
My father still must groan in Punic chains,
And waste the tedious hours in cruel bondage?
Days follow days, and years to years succeed,

And Rome forgets her hero, is content
That Regulus be a forgotten slave.
What is his crime? is it that he preferr'd
His country's profit to his children's good?
Is it th' unshaken firmness of his soul,
Just, uncorrupt, and, boasting, let me speak it,
Poor in the highest dignities of Rome?
O glorious poverty! illustrious crime!

MANLIUS
But know, Attilia—

ATTILIA
O have patience with me.
And can ungrateful Rome so soon forget?
Can those who breathe the air he breath'd forget
The great, the godlike virtues of my father?
There's not a part of Rome but speaks his praise.
The streets—through them the hero pass'd triumphant:
The Forum—there the Legislator plann'd
The wisest, purest laws:—the Senate House—
There spoke the patriot Roman—there his voice
Secur'd the public safety: Manlius, yes;
The wisdom of his councils match'd his valour.
Enter the Temples—mount the Capitol—
And tell me, Manlius, to what hand but his
They owe their trophies, and their ornaments.
Their foreign banners, and their boasted ensigns,
Tarentine, Punic, and Sicilian spoils?
Nay, e'en those lictors who precede thy steps,
This Consul's purple which invests thy limbs,
All, all were Regulus's, were my father's.
And yet this hero, this exalted patriot,
This man of virtue, this immortal Roman,
In base requital for his services,
Is left to linger out a life in chains,
No honours paid him but a daughter's tears.
O Rome! O Regulus! O thankless citizens!

MANLIUS
Just are thy tears:—thy father well deserves them;
But know thy censure is unjust, Attilia.
The fate of Regulus is felt by all:
We know and mourn the cruel woes he suffers
From barbarous Carthage.

ATTILIA
Manlius, you mistake;

Alas! it is not Carthage which is barbarous;
'Tis Rome, ungrateful Rome, is the barbarian;
Carthage but punishes a foe profess'd,
But Rome betrays her hero and her father:
Carthage remembers how he slew her sons,
But Rome forgets the blood he shed for her:
Carthage revenges an acknowledged foe,
But Rome, with basest perfidy, rewards
The glorious hand that bound her brow with laurels.
Which now is the barbarian, Rome or Carthage?

MANLIUS
What can be done?

ATTILIA
A woman shall inform you.
Convene the senate; let them strait propose
A ransom, or exchange for Regulus,
To Africa's ambassador. Do this,
And heaven's best blessings crown your days with peace.

MANLIUS
Thou speakest like a daughter, I, Attilia,
Must as a Consul act; I must consult
The good of Rome, and with her good, her glory.
Would it not tarnish her unspotted fame,
To sue to Carthage on the terms thou wishest?

ATTILIA
Ah! rather own thou'rt still my father's foe.

MANLIUS
Ungen'rous maid! no fault of mine concurr'd
To his destruction. 'Twas the chance of war.
Farewell! ere this the senate is assembled—
My presence is requir'd.—Speak to the fathers,
And try to soften their austerity;
My rigour they may render vain, for know,
I am Rome's Consul, not her King, Attilia.

[Exit **MANLIUS** with the **LICTORS**, &c.

ATTILIA (alone)
This flattering hope, alas! has prov'd abortive.
One Consul is our foe, the other absent.
What shall the sad Attilia next attempt?
Suppose I crave assistance from the people!
Ah! my unhappy father, on what hazards,

What strange vicissitudes, what various turns,
Thy life, thy liberty, thy all depends!

[Enter **BARCE** in haste.

BARCE
Ah, my Attilia!

ATTILIA
Whence this eager haste?

BARCE
Th' ambassador of Carthage is arriv'd.

ATTILIA
And why does that excite such wondrous transport?

BARCE
I bring another cause of greater still.

ATTILIA
Name it, my Barce.

BARCE
Regulus comes with him.

ATTILIA
My father! can it be?

BARCE
Thy father—Regulus.

ATTILIA
Thou art deceiv'd, or thou deceiv'st thy friend.

BARCE
Indeed I saw him not, but every tongue
Speaks the glad tidings.

[Enter **PUBLIUS**.

ATTILIA
See where Publius comes.

PUBLIUS
My sister, I'm transported! Oh, Attilia,
He's here, our father—Regulus is come!

ATTILIA I thank you, gods: O my full heart! where is he?
Hasten, my brother, lead, O lead me to him.

PUBLIUS
It is too soon: restrain thy fond impatience.
With Africa's ambassador he waits,
Until th' assembled senate give him audience.

ATTILIA
Where was he Publius when thou saw'st him first?

PUBLIUS
You know, in quality of Roman quæstor,
My duty 'tis to find a fit abode
For all ambassadors of foreign states.
Hearing the Carthaginian was arriv'd,
I hasten'd to the port, when, O just gods!
No foreigner, no foe, no African
Salutes my eye, but Regulus—my father!

ATTILIA
Oh mighty joy! too exquisite delight!
What said the hero? tell me, tell me all,
And ease my anxious breast.

PUBLIUS
Ere I arriv'd,
My father stood already on the shore,
Fixing his eyes with anxious eagerness,
As straining to descry the Capitol.
I saw, and flew with transport to embrace him,
Pronounc'd with wildest joy the name of father—
With reverence seiz'd his venerable hand,
And would have kiss'd it; when the awful hero,
With that stern grandeur which made Carthage tremble,
Drew back—stood all collected in himself,
And said austerely, Know, thou rash young man,
That slaves in Rome have not the rights of fathers.
Then ask'd, if yet the senate was assembled,
And where? which having heard, without indulging
The fond effusions of his soul, or mine,
He suddenly retir'd. I flew with speed
To find the Consul, but as yet success
Attends not my pursuit. Direct me to him.

BARCE
Publius, you'll find him in Bellona's temple.

ATTILIA
Then Regulus returns to Rome a slave!

PUBLIUS
Yes, but be comforted; I know he brings
Proposals for a peace; his will's his fate.

ATTILIA
Rome may, perhaps, refuse to treat of peace.

PUBLIUS
Didst thou behold the universal joy
At his return, thou wouldst not doubt success.
There's not a tongue in Rome but, wild with transport,
Proclaims aloud that Regulus is come;
The streets are filled with thronging multitudes,
Pressing with eager gaze to catch a look.
The happy man who can descry him first,
Points him to his next neighbour, he to his;
Then what a thunder of applause goes round;
What music to the ear of filial love!
Attilia! not a Roman eye was seen,
But shed pure tears of exquisite delight.
Judge of my feelings by thy own, my sister.
By the large measure of thy fond affection,
Judge mine.

ATTILIA
Where is Licinius? find him out;
My joy is incomplete till he partakes it.
When doubts and fears have rent my anxious heart,
In all my woes he kindly bore a part:
Felt all my sorrows with a soul sincere,
Sigh'd as I sigh'd, and number'd tear for tear:
Now favouring heav'n my ardent vows has blest,
He shall divide the transports of my breast.

[Exit **ATTILIA**

PUBLIUS
Barce, adieu!

BARCE
Publius, a moment hear me.
Know'st thou the name of Africa's ambassador?

PUBLIUS
Hamilcar.

BARCE
Son of Hanno?

PUBLIUS
Yes! the same.

BARCE
Ah me! Hamilcar!—How shall I support it!   [Aside.

PUBLIUS
Ah, charming maid! the blood forsakes thy cheek:
Is he the rival of thy Publius? speak,
And tell me all the rigour of my fate.

BARCE
Hear me, my Lord. Since I have been thy slave,
Thy goodness, and the friendship of Attilia,
Have soften'd all the horrors of my fate.
Till now I have not felt the weight of bondage.
Till now—ah, Publius!—think me not ungrateful,
I would not wrong thee—I will be sincere—
I will expose the weakness of my soul.
Know then, my Lord—how shall I tell thee all?

PUBLIUS
Stop, cruel maid, nor wound thy Publius more;
I dread the fatal frankness of thy words:
Spare me the pain of knowing I am scorn'd;
And if thy heart's devoted to another,
Yet do not tell it me; in tender pity
Do not, my fair, dissolve the fond illusion,
The dear delightful visions I have form'd
Of future joy, and fond exhaustless love.

[Exit **PUBLIUS**

BARCE (alone)
And shall I see him then, see my Hamilcar,
Pride of my soul, and lord of all my wishes?
The only man in all our burning Afric
Who ever taught my bosom how to love!
Down, foolish heart! be calm, my busy thoughts!
If at his name I feel these strange emotions,
How shall I see, how meet my conqueror?
O let not those presume to judge of joy
Who ne'er have felt the pangs which absence gives.
Such tender transport those alone can prove,

Who long, like me, have known disastrous love;
The tears that fell, the sighs that once were paid,
Like grateful incense on his altar laid;
The lambent flame rekindle, not destroy,
And woes remember'd heighten present joy.

[Exit.

ACT II

SCENE—The Inside of the Temple of Bellona

Seats for the **SENATORS** and **AMBASSADORS**—**LICTORS** guarding the entrance.

MANLIUS, PUBLIUS, and **SENATORS.**

MANLIUS
Let Regulus be sent for to our presence;
And with him the ambassador of Carthage.
Is it then true the foe would treat of peace?

PUBLIUS
They wish, at least, our captives were exchang'd,
And send my father to declare their wish:
If he obtain it, well: if not, then Regulus
Returns to meet the vengeance of the foe,
And pay for your refusal with his blood:
He ratified this treaty with his oath,
And ere he quitted Carthage, heard, unmov'd,
The dreadful preparations for his death,
Should he return. O, Romans! O, my countrymen!
Can you resign your hero to your foe?
Say, can you give up Regulus to Carthage?

MANLIUS
Peace, Publius, peace, for see thy father comes.

[Enter **HAMILCAR** and **REGULUS.**

HAMILCAR
Why dost thou stop? dost thou forget this temple?
I thought these walls had been well known to Regulus?

REGULUS
Hamilcar! I was thinking what I was
When last I saw them, and what now I am.

HAMILCAR (to the **CONSUL**)
Carthage by me to Rome this greeting sends,
That wearied out at length with bloody war,
If Rome inclines to peace she offers it.

MANLIUS We will at leisure answer thee. Be seated.
Come, Regulus, resume thine ancient place.

REGULUS (pointing to the **SENATORS**)
Who then are these?

MANLIUS
The Senators of Rome.

REGULUS
And who art thou?

MANLIUS
What meanst thou? I'm her Consul;
Hast thou so soon forgotten Manlius?

REGULUS
And shall a slave then have a place in Rome
Among her Consuls and her Senators?

MANLIUS
Yes!—For her heroes Rome forgets her laws;
Softens their harsh austerity for thee,
To whom she owes her conquests and her triumphs.

REGULUS
Rome may forget, but Regulus remembers.

MANLIUS
Was ever man so obstinately good? [Aside.

PUBLIUS (rising: To the **SENATORS**)
Fathers! your pardon. I can sit no longer.

REGULUS
Publius, what dost thou mean?

PUBLIUS
To do my duty:
Where Regulus must stand, shall Publius sit?

REGULUS

Alas! O Rome, how are thy manners chang'd!
When last I left thee, ere I sail'd for Afric,
It was a crime to think of private duties
When public cares requir'd attention.—Sit,
(To **PUBLIUS**)
And learn to occupy thy place with honour.

PUBLIUS
Forgive me, sir, if I refuse obedience:
My heart o'erflows with duty to my father.

REGULUS
Know, Publius, that duty's at an end;
Thy father died when he became a slave.

MANLIUS
Now urge thy suit, Hamilcar, we attend.

HAMILCAR
Afric hath chosen Regulus her messenger.
In him, both Carthage and Hamilcar speak.

MANLIUS (to **REGULUS**)
We are prepar'd to hear thee.

HAMILCAR (to **REGULUS**)
Ere thou speak'st,
Maturely weigh what thou hast sworn to do,
Should Rome refuse to treat with us of peace.

REGULUS
What I have sworn I will fulfil, Hamilcar.
Be satisfied.

PUBLIUS
Ye guardian gods of Rome,
With your own eloquence inspire him now!

REGULUS
Carthage by me this embassy has sent:
If Rome will leave her undisturb'd possession
Of all she now enjoys, she offers peace;
But if you rather wish protracted war,
Her next proposal is, exchange of captives;—
If you demand advice of Regulus,
Reject them both!

HAMILCAR

What dost thou mean?

PUBLIUS
My father!

MANLIUS
Exalted fortitude! I'm lost in wonder.   [Aside.

REGULUS
Romans! I will not idly spend my breath,
To show the dire effects of such a peace;
The foes who beg it, show their dread of war.

MANLIUS
But the exchange of prisoners thou proposest?

REGULUS
That artful scheme conceals some Punic fraud.

HAMILCAR
Roman, beware! hast thou so soon forgotten;

REGULUS
I will fulfil the treaty I have sworn to.

PUBLIUS
All will be ruin'd.

REGULUS
Conscript Fathers! hear me.—
Though this exchange teems with a thousand ills,
Yet 'tis th' example I would deprecate.
This treaty fix'd, Rome's honour is no more.
Should her degenerate sons be promis'd life,
Dishonest life, and worthless liberty,
Her glory, valour, military pride,
Her fame, her fortitude, her all were lost.
What honest captive of them all would wish
With shame to enter her imperial gates,
The flagrant scourge of slavery on his back?
None, none, my friends, would wish a fate so vile,
But those base cowards who resign'd their arms
Unstain'd with hostile blood, and poorly sued,
Through ignominious fear of death, for bondage;
The scorn, the laughter, of th' insulting foe.
O shame! shame! shame! eternal infamy!

MANLIUS

However hurtful this exchange may be,
The liberty, the life of Regulus,
More than compensates for it.

REGULUS
Thou art mistaken.—
This Regulus is a mere mortal man,
Yielding apace to all th' infirmities
Of weak, decaying nature.—I am old,
Nor can my future, feeble services
Assist my country much; but mark me well:
The young fierce heroes you'd restore to Carthage,
In lieu of this old man, are her chief bulwarks.
Fathers! in vig'rous youth this well-strung arm
Fought for my country, fought and conquer'd for her:
That was the time to prize its service high.
Now, weak and nerveless, let the foe possess it,
For it can harm them in the field no more.
Let Carthage have the poor degrading triumph
To close these failing eyes;—but, O my countrymen!
Check their vain hopes, and show aspiring Afric
That heroes are the common growth of Rome.

MANLIUS
Unequall'd fortitude.

PUBLIUS
O fatal virtue!

HAMILCAR
What do I hear? this constancy confounds me.

MANLIUS (to the **SENATORS**)
Let honour be the spring of all our actions,
Not interest, Fathers. Let no selfish views
Preach safety at the price of truth and justice.

REGULUS
If Rome would thank me, I will teach her how.
—Know, Fathers, that these savage Africans
Thought me so base, so very low of soul,
That the poor wretched privilege of breathing,
Would force me to betray my country to them.
Have these barbarians any tortures left
To match the cruelty of such a thought?
Revenge me, Fathers! and I'm still a Roman.
Arm, arm yourselves, prepare your citizens,
Snatch your imprison'd eagles from their fanes,

Fly to the shores of Carthage, force her gates,
Dye every Roman sword in Punic blood—
And do such deeds—that when I shall return,
(As I have sworn, and am resolv'd to do,)
I may behold with joy, reflected back,
The terrors of your rage in the dire visages
Of my astonish'd executioners.

HAMILCAR
Surprise has chill'd my blood! I'm lost in wonder!

PUBLIUS
Does no one answer? must my father perish?

MANLIUS
Romans, we must defer th' important question;
Maturest councils must determine on it.
Rest we awhile:—Nature requires some pause
From high-rais'd admiration. Thou, Hamilcar,
Shalt shortly know our final resolution.
Meantime, we go to supplicate the gods.

REGULUS
Have you a doubt remaining? Manlius, speak.

MANLIUS
Yes, Regulus, I think the danger less
To lose th' advantage thy advice suggests,
Than would accrue to Rome in losing thee,
Whose wisdom might direct, whose valour guard her.
Athirst for glory, thou wouldst rush on death,
And for thy country's sake wouldst greatly perish.
Too vast a sacrifice thy zeal requires,
For Rome must bleed when Regulus expires.

[Exeunt **CONSUL** and **SENATORS**.

[**REGULUS, PUBLIUS, HAMILCAR**; to them

[Enter **ATTILIA** and **LICINIUS**.

HAMILCAR
Does Regulus fulfil his promise thus?

REGULUS
I've promis'd to return, and I will do it.

ATTILIA

My father! think a moment.

LICINIUS
Ah! my friend!

LICINIUS and **ATTILIA**
O by this hand we beg—

REGULUS
Away! no more.
Thanks to Rome's guardian gods I'm yet a slave!
And will be still a slave to make Rome free!

ATTILIA
Was the exchange refus'd? Oh ease my fears.

REGULUS
Publius! conduct Hamilcar and myself
To that abode thou hast for each provided.

ATTILIA
A foreign residence? a strange abode?
And will my father spurn his household gods?

PUBLIUS
My sire a stranger?—Will he taste no more
The smiling blessings of his cheerful home?

REGULUS
Dost thou not know the laws of Rome forbid
A foe's ambassador within her gates?

PUBLIUS
This rigid law does not extend to thee.

REGULUS
Yes; did it not alike extend to all,
'Twere tyranny.—The law rights every man,
But favours none.

ATTILIA
Then, O my father,
Allow thy daughter to partake thy fate!

REGULUS
Attilia! no. The present exigence
Demands far other thoughts, than the soft cares,
The fond effusions, the delightful weakness,

The dear affections 'twixt the child and parent.

ATTILIA
How is my father chang'd, from what I've known him!

REGULUS
The fate of Regulus is chang'd, not Regulus.
I am the same; in laurels or in chains
'Tis the same principle; the same fix'd soul,
Unmov'd itself, though circumstances change.
The native vigour of the free-born mind
Still struggles with, still conquers adverse fortune;
Soars above chains, invincible though vanquish'd.

[Exeunt **REGULUS** and **PUBLIUS**.

[**ATTILIA, HAMILCAR** going; enter **BARCE**.

BARCE
Ah! my Hamilcar.

HAMILCAR
Ah! my long-lost Barce:
Again I lose thee; Regulus rejects
Th' exchange of prisoners Africa proposes.
My heart's too full.—Oh, I have much to say!

BARCE
Yet you unkindly leave me, and say nothing.

HAMILCAR
Ah! didst thou love as thy Hamilcar loves,
Words were superfluous; in my eyes, my Barce,
Thou'dst read the tender eloquence of love,
Th' uncounterfeited language of my heart.
A single look betrays the soul's soft feelings,
And shows imperfect speech of little worth.

[Exit **HAMILCAR**.

ATTILIA
My father then conspires his own destruction,
Is it not so?

BARCE
Indeed I fear it much;
But as the senate has not yet resolv'd,
There is some room for hope: lose not a moment;

And, ere the Conscript Fathers are assembled,
Try all the powers of winning eloquence,
Each gentle art of feminine persuasion,
The love of kindred, and the faith of friends,
To bend the rigid Romans to thy purpose.

ATTILIA
Yes, Barce, I will go; I will exert
My little pow'r, though hopeless of success.
Undone Attilia! fall'n from hope's gay heights
Down the dread precipice of deep despair.
So some tir'd mariner the coast espies,
And his lov'd home explores with straining eyes;
Prepares with joy to quit the treacherous deep,
Hush'd every wave, and every wind asleep;
But ere he lands upon the well-known shore,
Wild storms arise, and furious billows roar,
Tear the fond wretch from all his hopes away,
And drive his shatter'd bark again to sea.

ACT III

SCENE—A Portico of a Palace Without the Gates of Rome—The Abode of the Carthaginian
Ambassador.

Enter **REGULUS** and **PUBLIUS** meeting.

REGULUS
Ah! Publius here at such a time as this?
Know'st thou th' important question that the Senate
This very hour debate?—Thy country's glory,
Thy father's honour, and the public good?
Dost thou know this and fondly linger here?

PUBLIUS
They're not yet met, my father.

REGULUS
Haste—away—
Support my counsel in th' assembled Senate,
Confirm their wav'ring virtue by thy courage,
And Regulus shall glory in his boy.

PUBLIUS
Ah! spare thy son the most ungrateful task.
What!—supplicate the ruin of my father?

REGULUS

The good of Rome can never hurt her sons.

PUBLIUS

In pity to thy children, spare thyself.

REGULUS

Dost thou then think that mine's a frantic bravery?
That Regulus would rashly seek his fate?
Publius! how little dost thou know thy sire!
Misjudging youth! learn, that like other men,
I shun the evil, and I seek the good;
But that I find in guilt, and this in virtue.
Were it not guilt, guilt of the blackest die,
Even to think of freedom at th' expense
Of my dear bleeding country? To me, therefore,
Freedom and life would be the heaviest evils;
But to preserve that country, to restore her,
To heal her wounds though at the price of life,
Or what is dearer far, the price of liberty,
Is virtue—therefore slavery and death
Are Regulus's good—his wish—his choice.

PUBLIUS

Yet sure our country—

REGULUS

Is a whole, my Publius,
Of which we all are parts; nor should a citizen
Regard his interests as distinct from hers;
No hopes or fears should touch his patriot soul,
But what affect her honour or her shame.
E'en when in hostile fields he bleeds to save her,
'Tis not his blood he loses, 'tis his country's;
He only pays her back a debt he owes.
To her he's bound for birth and education:
Her laws secure him from domestic feuds,
And from the foreign foe her arms protect him.
She lends him honours, dignity, and rank,
His wrongs revenges, and his merit pays;
And like a tender and indulgent mother,
Loads him with comforts, and would make his state
As blest as nature and the gods design'd it.
Such gifts, my son, have their alloy of pain;
And let th' unworthy wretch who will not bear
His portion of the public burden lose
Th' advantages it yields;—let him retire

From the dear blessings of a social life,
And from the sacred laws which guard those blessings;
Renounce the civilis'd abodes of man,
With kindred brutes one common shelter seek
In horrid wilds, and dens, and dreary caves,
And with their shaggy tenants share the spoil;
Or if the savage hunters miss their prey,
From scatter'd acorns pick a scanty meal;—
Far from the sweet civilities of life;
There let him live and vaunt his wretched freedom:
While we, obedient to the laws that guard us,
Guard them, and live or die as they decree.

PUBLIUS

With reverence and astonishment I hear thee!
Thy words, my father, have convinc'd my reason,
But cannot touch my heart:—nature denies
Obedience so repugnant. I'm a son.

REGULUS

A poor excuse, unworthy of a Roman!
Brutus, Virginius, Manlius—they were fathers.

PUBLIUS

'Tis true, they were; but this heroic greatness,
This glorious elevation of the soul,
Has been confin'd to fathers.—Rome, till now,
Boasts not a son of such unnatural virtue,
Who, spurning all the powerful ties of blood,
Has labour'd to procure his father's death.

REGULUS

Then be the first to give the great example—
Go, hasten; be thyself that son, my Publius.

PUBLIUS

My father! ah!—

REGULUS

Publius, no more; begone—
Attend the Senate—let me know my fate;
'Twill be more glorious if announc'd by thee.

PUBLIUS

Too much, too much thy rigid virtue claims
From thy unhappy son. Oh, nature, nature!

REGULUS

Publius! am I a stranger, or thy father?
In either case an obvious duty waits thee:
If thou regard'st me as an alien here,
Learn to prefer to mine the good of Rome;
If as a father—reverence my commands.

PUBLIUS
Ah! couldst thou look into my inmost soul,
And see how warm it burns with love and duty,
Thou would'st abate the rigour of thy words.

REGULUS
Could I explore the secrets of thy breast,
The virtue I would wish should flourish there
Were fortitude, not weak, complaining love.

PUBLIUS
If thou requir'st my blood, I'll shed it all;
But when thou dost enjoin the harsher task
That I should labour to procure thy death,
Forgive thy son—he has not so much virtue.

[Exit **PUBLIUS**.

REGULUS
Th' important hour draws on, and now my soul
Loses her wonted calmness, lest the Senate
Should doubt what answer to return to Carthage.
O ye protecting deities of Rome!
Ye guardian gods! look down propitious on her,
Inspire her Senate with your sacred wisdom,
And call up all that's Roman in their souls!

[Enter **MANLIUS** speaking.

See that the lictors wait, and guard the entrance—
Take care that none intrude.

REGULUS
Ah! Manlius here?
What can this mean?

MANLIUS
Where, where is Regulus?
The great, the godlike, the invincible?
Oh, let me strain the hero to my breast.—

REGULUS (avoiding him)

Manlius, stand off, remember I'm a slave!
And thou Rome's Consul.

MANLIUS
I am something more:
I am a man enamour'd of thy virtues;
Thy fortitude and courage have subdued me.
I was thy rival—I am now thy friend;
Allow me that distinction, dearer far
Than all the honours Rome can give without it.

REGULUS
This is the temper still of noble minds,
And these the blessings of an humble fortune.
Had I not been a slave, I ne'er had gain'd
The treasure of thy friendship.

MANLIUS
I confess,
Thy grandeur cast a veil before my eyes,
Which thy reverse of fortune has remov'd.
Oft have I seen thee on the day of triumph,
A conqueror of nations, enter Rome;
Now, thou hast conquer'd fortune, and thyself.
Thy laurels oft have mov'd my soul to envy,
Thy chains awaken my respect, my reverence;
Then Regulus appear'd a hero to me,
He rises now a god.

REGULUS
Manlius, enough.
Cease thy applause; 'tis dang'rous; praise like thine
Might tempt the most severe and cautious virtue.
Bless'd be the gods, who gild my latter days
With the bright glory of the Consul's friendship!

MANLIUS
Forbid it, Jove! said'st thou thy latter days?
May gracious heav'n to a far distant hour
Protract thy valued life! Be it my care
To crown the hopes of thy admiring country,
By giving back her long-lost hero to her.
I will exert my power to bring about
Th' exchange of captives Africa proposes.

REGULUS
Manlius, and is it thus, is this the way
Thou dost begin to give me proofs of friendship?

Ah! if thy love be so destructive to me,
What would thy hatred be? Mistaken Consul!
Shall I then lose the profit of my wrongs?
Be thus defrauded of the benefit
I vainly hop'd from all my years of bondage?
I did not come to show my chains to Rome,
To move my country to a weak compassion;
I came to save her honour, to preserve her
From tarnishing her glory; came to snatch her
From offers so destructive to her fame.
O Manlius! either give me proofs more worthy
A Roman's friendship, or renew thy hate.

MANLIUS
Dost thou not know, that this exchange refus'd,
Inevitable death must be thy fate?

REGULUS
And has the name of death such terror in it,
To strike with dread the mighty soul of Manlius?
'Tis not to-day I learn that I am mortal.
The foe can only take from Regulus
What wearied nature would have shortly yielded;
It will be now a voluntary gift,
'Twould then become a tribute seiz'd, not offer'd.
Yes, Manlius, tell the world that as I liv'd
For Rome alone, when I could live no longer,
'Twas my last care how, dying, to assist,
To save that country I had liv'd to serve.

MANLIUS
O unexampled worth! O godlike Regulus!
Thrice happy Rome! unparalleled in heroes!
Hast thou then sworn, thou awfully good man,
Never to bless the Consul with thy friendship?

REGULUS
If thou wilt love me, love me like a Roman.
These are the terms on which I take thy friendship.
We both must make a sacrifice to Rome,
I of my life, and thou of Regulus:
One must resign his being, one his friend.
It is but just, that what procures our country
Such real blessings, such substantial good,
Should cost thee something—I shall lose but little.
Go then, my friend! but promise, ere thou goest,
With all the Consular authority,
Thou wilt support my counsel in the Senate.

If thou art willing to accept these terms,
With transport I embrace thy proffer'd friendship.

MANLIUS (after a pause)
Yes, I do promise.

REGULUS
Bounteous gods, I thank you!
Ye never gave, in all your round of blessing,
A gift so greatly welcome to my soul,
As Manlius' friendship on the terms of honour!

MANLIUS
Immortal Powers! why am not I a slave?
By heav'n! I almost envy thee thy bonds.

REGULUS
My friend, there's not a moment to be lost;
Ere this, perhaps, the Senate is assembled.
To thee, and to thy virtues, I commit
The dignity of Rome—my peace and honour.

MANLIUS
Illustrious man, farewell!

REGULUS
Farewell, my friend!

MANLIUS
The sacred flame thou hast kindled in my soul
Glows in each vein, trembles in every nerve,
And raises me to something more than man.
My blood is fir'd with virtue, and with Rome,
And every pulse beats an alarm to glory.
Who would not spurn a sceptre when compar'd
With chains like thine? Thou man of every virtus,
O, farewell! may all the gods protect and bless thee.

[Exit **MANLIUS**.

[Enter **LICINIUS**.

REGULUS
Now I begin to live; propitious heaven
Inclines to favour me.—Licinius here?

LICINIUS
With joy, my honour'd friend, I seek thy presence.

REGULUS
And why with joy?

LICINIUS
Because my heart once more
Beats high with flattering hope. In thy great cause
I have been labouring.

REGULUS
Say'st thou in my cause?

LICINIUS
In thine and Rome's. Does it excite thy wonder?
Couldst thou, then, think so poorly of Licinius,
That base ingratitude could find a place
Within his bosom?—Can I, then, forget
Thy thousand acts of friendship to my youth?
Forget them, too, at that important moment
When most I might assist thee?—Regulus,
Thou wast my leader, general, father—all.
Didst thou not teach me early how to tread
The path of glory; point the way thyself,
And bid me follow thee?

REGULUS
But say, Licinius,
What hast thou done to serve me?

LICINIUS
I have defended
Thy liberty and life!

REGULUS
Ah! speak—explain.—

LICINIUS
Just as the Fathers were about to meet,
I hasten'd to the temple—at the entrance
Their passage I retarded by the force
Of strong entreaty: then address'd myself
So well to each, that I from each obtain'd
A declaration, that his utmost power
Should be exerted for thy life and freedom.

REGULUS
Great gods! what do I hear? Licinius, too?

LICINIUS
Not he alone; no, 'twere indeed unjust
To rob the fair Attilia of her claim
To filial merit.—What I could, I did.
But she—thy charming daughter—heav'n and earth,
What did she not to save her father?

REGULUS
Who?

LICINIUS
Attilia, thy belov'd—thy age's darling!
Was ever father bless'd with such a child?
Gods! how her looks took captive all who saw her!
How did her soothing eloquence subdue
The stoutest hearts of Rome! How did she rouse
Contending passions in the breasts of all!
How sweetly temper dignity with grief!
With what a soft, inimitable grace
She prais'd, reproach'd, entreated, flatter'd, sooth'd.

REGULUS
What said the Senators?

LICINIUS
What could they say?
Who could resist the lovely conqueror?
See where she comes—Hope dances in her eyes,
And lights up all her beauties into smiles.

[Enter **ATTILIA**.

ATTILIA
Once more, my dearest father—

REGULUS
Ah, presume not
To call me by that name. For know, Attilia,
I number thee among the foes of Regulus.

ATTILIA
What do I hear? thy foe? my father's foe?

REGULUS
His worst of foes—the murd'rer of his glory.

ATTILIA
Ah! is it then a proof of enmity

To wish thee all the good the gods can give thee,
To yield my life, if needful, for thy service?

REGULUS
Thou rash, imprudent girl! thou little know'st
The dignity and weight of public cares.
Who made a weak and inexperienc'd woman
The arbiter of Regulus's fate?

LICINIUS
For pity's sake, my Lord!

REGULUS
Peace, peace, young man!
Her silence better than thy language pleads.
That bears at least the semblance of repentance.
Immortal Powers!—a daughter and a Roman!

ATTILIA
Because I am a daughter, I presum'd—

LICINIUS
Because I am a Roman, I aspired
T' oppose th' inhuman rigour of thy fate.

REGULUS
No more, Licinius. How can he be call'd
A Roman who would live in infamy?
Or how can she be Regulus's daughter
Whose coward mind wants fortitude and honour?
Unhappy children! now you make me feel
The burden of my chains: your feeble souls
Have made me know I am indeed a slave.

[Exit **REGULUS**.

ATTILIA
Tell me, Licinius, and, oh! tell me truly,
If thou believ'st, in all the round of time,
There ever breath'd a maid so truly wretched?
To weep, to mourn a father's cruel fate—
To love him with soul-rending tenderness—
To know no peace by day or rest by night—
To bear a bleeding heart in this poor bosom,
Which aches, and trembles but to think he suffers:
This is my crime—in any other child
'Twould be a merit.

LICINIUS

Oh! my best Attilia,
Do not repent thee of the pious deed:
It was a virtuous error. That in us
Is a just duty, which the god-like soul
Of Regulus would think a shameful weakness.
If the contempt of life in him be virtue,
It were in us a crime to let him perish.
Perhaps at last he may consent to live:
He then will thank us for our cares to save him:
Let not his anger fright thee. Though our love
Offend him now, yet, when his mighty soul
Is reconcil'd to life, he will not chide us.
The sick man loathes, and with reluctance takes
The remedy by which his health's restor'd.

ATTILIA

Licinius! his reproaches wound my soul.
I cannot live and bear his indignation.

LICINIUS

Would my Attilia rather lose her father
Than, by offending him, preserve his life?

ATTILIA

Ah! no. If he but live, I am contented.

LICINIUS

Yes, he shall live, and we again be bless'd;
Then dry thy tears, and let those lovely orbs
Beam with their wonted lustre on Licinius,
Who lives but in the sunshine of thy smiles.

[Exit **LICINIUS**.

ATTILIA (alone)

O Fortune, Fortune, thou capricious goddess!
Thy frowns and favours have alike no bounds:
Unjust, or prodigal in each extreme.
When thou wouldst humble human vanity,
By singling out a wretch to bear thy wrath,
Thou crushest him with anguish to excess:
If thou wouldst bless, thou mak'st the happiness
Too poignant for his giddy sense to bear.—
Immortal gods, who rule the fates of men,
Preserve my father! bless him, bless him, heav'n!
If your avenging thunderbolts must fall,
Strike here—this bosom will invite the blow,

And thank you for it: but in mercy spare,
Oh! spare his sacred, venerable head:
Respect in him an image of yourselves;
And leave a world, who wants it, an example
Of courage, wisdom, constancy and truth.
Yet if, Eternal Powers who rule this ball!
You have decreed that Regulus must fall;
Teach me to yield to your divine command,
And meekly bow to your correcting hand;
Contented to resign, or pleas'd receive,
What wisdom may withhold, or mercy give.

[Exit **ATTILIA**.

ACT IV

SCENE—A Gallery in the Ambassador's Palace

REGULUS (alone)
Be calm, my soul! what strange emotions shake thee?
Emotions thou hast never felt till now.
Thou hast defied the dangers of the deep,
Th' impetuous hurricane, the thunder's roar,
And all the terrors of the various war;
Yet, now thou tremblest, now thou stand'st dismay'd,
With fearful expectation of thy fate.—
Yes—thou hast amplest reason for thy fears;
For till this hour, so pregnant with events,
Thy fame and glory never were at stake.
Soft—let me think—what is this thing call'd glory?
'Tis the soul's tyrant, that should be dethron'd,
And learn subjection like her other passions!
Ah! no! 'tis false: this is the coward's plea;
The lazy language of refining vice.
That man was born in vain, whose wish to serve
Is circumscrib'd within the wretched bounds
Of self—a narrow, miserable sphere!
Glory exalts, enlarges, dignifies,
Absorbs the selfish in the social claims,
And renders man a blessing to mankind.—
It is this principle, this spark of deity,
Rescues debas'd humanity from guilt,
And elevates it by her strong excitements:—
It takes off sensibility from pain,
From peril fear, plucks out the sting from death,
Changes ferocious into gentle manners,

And teaches men to imitate the gods.
It shows—but see, alas! where Publius comes.
Ah! he advances with a down-cast eye,
And step irresolute—

[Enter **PUBLIUS**.

REGULUS
My Publius, welcome!
What tidings dost thou bring? what says the Senate?
Is yet my fate determin'd? quickly tell me.—

PUBLIUS
I cannot speak, and yet, alas! I must.

REGULUS
Tell me the whole.—

PUBLIUS
Would I were rather dumb!

REGULUS
Publius, no more delay:—I charge thee speak.

PUBLIUS
The Senate has decreed thou shalt depart.

REGULUS
Genius of Rome! thou hast at last prevail'd—
I thank the gods, I have not liv'd in vain!
Where is Hamilcar?—find him—let us go,
For Regulus has nought to do in Rome;
I have accomplished her important work,
And must depart.

PUBLIUS
Ah, my unhappy father!

REGULUS
Unhappy, Publius! didst thou say unhappy?
Does he, does that bless'd man deserve this name,
Who to his latest breath can serve his country?

PUBLIUS
Like thee, my father, I adore my country,
Yet weep with anguish o'er thy cruel chains.

REGULUS

Dost thou not know that life's a slavery?
The body is the chain that binds the soul;
A yoke that every mortal must endure.
Wouldst thou lament—lament the general fate,
The chain that nature gives, entail'd on all,
Not these I wear?

PUBLIUS
Forgive, forgive my sorrows:
I know, alas! too well, those fell barbarians
Intend thee instant death.

REGULUS
So shall my life
And servitude together have an end.—
Publius, farewell; nay, do not follow me.—

PUBLIUS
Alas! my father, if thou ever lov'dst me,
Refuse me not the mournful consolation
To pay the last sad offices of duty
I e'er can show thee.—

REGULUS
No!—thou canst fulfil
Thy duty to thy father in a way
More grateful to him: I must strait embark.
Be it meanwhile thy pious care to keep
My lov'd Attilia from a sight, I fear,
Would rend her gentle heart.—Her tears, my son,
Would dim the glories of thy father's triumph.
Her sinking spirits are subdu'd by grief.
And should her sorrows pass the bounds of reason,
Publius, have pity on her tender age,
Compassionate the weakness of her sex;
We must not hope to find in her soft soul
The strong exertion of a manly courage.—
Support her fainting spirit, and instruct her,
By thy example, how a Roman ought
To bear misfortune. Oh, indulge her weakness!
And be to her the father she will lose.
I leave my daughter to thee—I do more—
I leave to thee the conduct of—thyself.
—Ah, Publius! I perceive thy courage fails—
I see the quivering lip, the starting tear:—
That lip, that tear calls down my mounting soul.
Resume thyself—Oh, do not blast my hope!
Yes—I'm compos'd—thou wilt not mock my age—

Thou art—thou art a Roman—and my son.

[Exit.

PUBLIUS
And is he gone?—now be thyself, my soul—
Hard is the conflict, but the triumph glorious.
Yes.—I must conquer these too tender feelings;
The blood that fills these veins demands it of me;
My father's great example too requires it.
Forgive me Rome, and glory, if I yielded
To nature's strong attack:—I must subdue it.
Now, Regulus, I feel I am thy son.

[Enter **ATTILIA** and **BARCE**.

ATTILIA
My brother, I'm distracted, wild with fear—
Tell me, O tell me, what I dread to know—
Is it then true?—I cannot speak—my father?

BARCE
May we believe the fatal news?

PUBLIUS
Yes, Barce,
It is determin'd. Regulus must go.

ATTILIA
Immortal Powers!—What say'st thou?

BARCE
Can it be?
Thou canst not mean it.

ATTILIA
Then you've all betray'd me.

PUBLIUS Thy grief avails not.

[Enter **HAMILCAR** and **LICINIUS**.

BARCE
Pity us, Hamilcar!

ATTILIA
Oh, help, Licinius, help the lost Attilia!

HAMILCAR
My Barce! there's no hope.

LICINIUS
Ah! my fair mourner,
All's lost.

ATTILIA
What all, Licinius? said'st thou all?
Not one poor glimpse of comfort left behind?
Tell me, at least, where Regulus is gone:
The daughter shall partake the father's chains,
And share the woes she knew not to prevent.

[Going.

PUBLIUS
What would thy wild despair? Attilia, stay,
Thou must not follow; this excess of grief
Would much offend him.

ATTILIA
Dost thou hope to stop me?

PUBLIUS
I hope thou wilt resume thy better self,
And recollect thy father will not bear—

ATTILIA
I only recollect I am a daughter,
A poor, defenceless, helpless, wretched daughter!
Away—and let me follow.

PUBLIUS
No, my sister.

ATTILIA
Detain me not—Ah! while thou hold'st me here,
He goes, and I shall never see him more.

BARCE
My friend, be comforted, he cannot go
Whilst here Hamilcar stays.

ATTILIA
O Barce, Barce!
Who will advise, who comfort, who assist me?
Hamilcar, pity me.—Thou wilt not answer?

HAMILCAR

Rage and astonishment divide my soul.

ATTILIA

Licinius, wilt thou not relieve my sorrows?

LICINIUS

Yes, at my life's expense, my heart's best treasure,
Wouldst thou instruct me how.

ATTILIA

My brother, too—
Ah! look with mercy on thy sister's woes!

PUBLIUS

I will at least instruct thee how to bear them.
My sister—yield thee to thy adverse fate;
Think of thy father, think of Regulus;
Has he not taught thee how to brave misfortune?
'Tis but by following his illustrious steps
Thou e'er canst merit to be call'd his daughter.

ATTILIA

And is it thus thou dost advise thy sister?
Are these, ye gods, the feelings of a son?
Indifference here becomes impiety—
Thy savage heart ne'er felt the dear delights
Of filial tenderness—the thousand joys
That flow from blessing and from being bless'd!
No—didst thou love thy father as I love him,
Our kindred souls would be in unison;
And all my sighs be echoed back by thine.
Thou wouldst—alas!—I know not what I say.—
Forgive me, Publius,—but indeed, my brother,
I do not understand this cruel coldness.

HAMILCAR

Thou may'st not—but I understand it well.
His mighty soul, full as to thee it seems
Of Rome, and glory—is enamour'd—caught—
Enraptur'd with the beauties of fair Barce.—
She stays behind if Regulus departs.
Behold the cause of all the well-feign'd virtue
Of this mock patriot—curst dissimulation!

PUBLIUS

And canst thou entertain such vile suspicions?

Gods! what an outrage to a son like me!

HAMILCAR
Yes, Roman! now I see thee as thou art,
Thy naked soul divested of its veil,
Its specious colouring, its dissembled virtues:
Thou hast plotted with the Senate to prevent
Th' exchange of captives. All thy subtle arts,
Thy smooth inventions, have been set to work—
The base refinements of your polish'd land.

PUBLIUS (Contemptuously)
In truth the doubt is worthy of an African.

HAMILCAR
I know.—

PUBLIUS
Peace, Carthaginian, peace, and hear me,
Dost thou not know, that on the very man
Thou hast insulted, Barce's fate depends?

HAMILCAR
Too well I know, the cruel chance of war
Gave her, a blooming captive, to thy mother;
Who, dying, left the beauteous prize to thee.

PUBLIUS
Now, see the use a Roman makes of power.
Heav'n is my witness how I lov'd the maid!
Oh, she was dearer to my soul than light!
Dear as the vital stream that feeds my heart!
But know my honour's dearer than my love.
I do not even hope thou wilt believe me;
Thy brutal soul, as savage as thy clime,
Can never taste those elegant delights,
Those pure refinements, love and glory yield.
'Tis not to thee I stoop for vindication,
Alike to me thy friendship or thy hate;
But to remove from others a pretence
For branding Publius with the name of villain;
That they may see no sentiment but honour
Informs this bosom—Barce, thou art free.
Thou hast my leave with him to quit this shore.
Now learn, barbarian, how a Roman loves!

[Exit.

BARCE
He cannot mean it!

HAMILCAR
Oh, exalted virtue!
Which challenges esteem though from a foe.

[Looking after **PUBLIUS**.

ATTILIA
Ah! cruel Publius, wilt thou leave me thus?
Thus leave thy sister?

BARCE
Didst thou hear, Hamilcar?
Oh, didst thou hear the god-like youth resign me?

[**HAMILCAR** and **LICINIUS** seem lost in thought.

HAMILCAR
Farewell, I will return.

LICINIUS
Farewell, my love! [To **ATTILIA**.

BARCE
Hamilcar, where—

ATTILIA [To **LICINIUS**.
Alas! where art thou going?

LICINIUS
If possible, to save the life of Regulus.

ATTILIA
But by what means?—Ah! how canst thou effect it?

LICINIUS
Since the disease so desperate is become,
We must apply a desperate remedy.

HAMILCAR (after a long pause)
Yes—I will mortify this generous foe;
I'll be reveng'd upon this stubborn Roman;
Not by defiance bold, or feats of arms,
But by a means more sure to work its end;
By emulating his exalted worth,
And showing him a virtue like his own;

Such a refin'd revenge as noble minds
Alone can practise, and alone can feel.

ATTILIA
If thou wilt go, Licinius, let Attilia
At least go with thee.

LICINIUS
No, my gentle love,
Too much I prize thy safety and thy peace.
Let me entreat thee, stay with Barce here
Till our return.

ATTILIA
Then, ere ye go, in pity
Explain the latent purpose of your souls.

LICINIUS [To **HAMILCAR** as he goes out.
Soon shalt thou know it all—Farewell! farewell!
Let us keep Regulus in Rome, or die.

HAMILCAR
Yes.—These smooth, polish'd Romans shall confess
The soil of Afric, too, produces heroes.
What, though our pride, perhaps, be less than theirs,
Our virtue may be equal: they shall own
The path of honour's not unknown to Carthage,
Nor, as they arrogantly think, confin'd
To their proud Capitol:—Yes—they shall learn
The gods look down on other climes than theirs.

[Exit.

ATTILIA
What gone, both gone? What can I think or do?
Licinius leaves me, led by love and virtue,
To rouse the citizens to war and tumult,
Which may be fatal to himself and Rome,
And yet, alas! not serve my dearest father.
Protecting deities! preserve them both!

BARCE
Nor is thy Barce more at ease, my friend;
I dread the fierceness of Hamilcar's courage:
Rous'd by the grandeur of thy brother's deed,
And stung by his reproaches, his great soul
Will scorn to be outdone by him in glory.
Yet, let us rise to courage and to life,

Forget the weakness of our helpless sex,
And mount above these coward woman's fears.
Hope dawns upon my mind—my prospect clears,
And every cloud now brightens into day.

ATTILIA

How different are our souls! Thy sanguine temper,
Flush'd with the native vigour of thy soil,
Supports thy spirits; while the sad Attilia,
Sinking with more than all her sex's fears,
Sees not a beam of hope; or, if she sees it,
'Tis not the bright, warm splendour of the sun;
It is a sickly and uncertain glimmer
Of instantaneous lightning passing by.
It shows, but not diminishes, the danger,
And leaves my poor benighted soul as dark
As it had never shone.

BARCE

Come, let us go.
Yes, joys unlook'd-for now shall gild thy days,
And brighter suns reflect propitious rays.

[Exeunt.

SCENE—A Hall Looking Towards the Garden

Enter **REGULUS**, speaking to one of **HAMILCAR'S ATTENDENTS**.

Where's your Ambassador? where is Hamilcar?
Ere this he doubtless knows the Senate's will.
Go, seek him out—Tell him we must depart—
Rome has no hope for him, or wish for me.
Longer delay were criminal in both.

[Enter **MANLIUS**.

REGULUS

He comes. The Consul comes! my noble friend!
O let me strain thee to this grateful heart,
And thank thee for the vast, vast debt I owe thee!
But for thy friendship I had been a wretch—
Had been compell'd to shameful liberty.
To thee I owe the glory of these chains,
My faith inviolate, my fame preserv'd,
My honour, virtue, glory, bondage,—all!

MANLIUS
But we shall lose thee, so it is decreed—
Thou must depart?

REGULUS
Because I must depart
You will not lose me; I were lost, indeed,
Did I remain in Rome.

MANLIUS
Ah! Regulus,
Why, why so late do I begin to love thee?
Alas! why have the adverse fates decreed
I ne'er must give thee other proofs of friendship,
Than those so fatal and so full of woe?

REGULUS
Thou hast perform'd the duties of a friend;
Of a just, faithful, Roman, noble friend:
Yet, generous as thou art, if thou constrain me
To sink beneath a weight of obligation,
I could—yes, Manlius—I could ask still more.

MANLIUS
Explain thyself.

REGULUS
I think I have fulfill'd
The various duties of a citizen;
Nor have I aught beside to do for Rome.
Now, nothing for the public good remains!
Manlius, I recollect I am a father!
My Publius! my Attilia! ah! my friend,
They are—(forgive the weakness of a parent)
To my fond heart dear as the drops that warm it.
Next to my country they're my all of life;
And, if a weak old man be not deceiv'd,
They will not shame that country. Yes, my friend,
The love of virtue blazes in their souls.
As yet these tender plants are immature,
And ask the fostering hand of cultivation:
Heav'n, in its wisdom, would not let their father
Accomplish this great work.—To thee, my friend,
The tender parent delegates the trust:
Do not refuse a poor man's legacy;
I do bequeath my orphans to thy love—
If thou wilt kindly take them to thy bosom,

Their loss will be repaid with usury.
Oh, let the father owe his glory to thee,
The children their protection!

MANLIUS
Regulus,
With grateful joy my heart accepts the trust:
Oh, I will shield, with jealous tenderness,
The precious blossoms from a blasting world.
In me thy children shall possess a father,
Though not as worthy, yet as fond as thee.
The pride be mine to fill their youthful breasts
With ev'ry virtue—'twill not cost me much:
I shall have nought to teach, nor they to learn,
But the great history of their god-like sire.

REGULUS
I will not hurt the grandeur of thy virtue,
By paying thee so poor a thing as thanks.
Now all is over, and I bless the gods,
I've nothing more to do.

[Enter **PUBLIUS** in haste.

PUBLIUS
O Regulus!

REGULUS
Say what has happened?

PUBLIUS
Rome is in a tumult—
There's scarce a citizen but runs to arms—
They will not let thee go.

REGULUS
Is't possible?
Can Rome so far forget her dignity
As to desire this infamous exchange?
I blush to think it!

PUBLIUS
Ah! not so, my father.
Rome cares not for the peace, nor for th' exchange;
She only wills that Regulus shall stay.

REGULUS
How, stay? my oath—my faith—my honour! ah!

Do they forget?

PUBLIUS
No: every man exclaims
That neither faith nor honour should be kept
With Carthaginian perfidy and fraud.

REGULUS
Gods! gods! on what vile principles they reason!
Can guilt in Carthage palliate guilt in Rome,
Or vice in one absolve it in another?
Ah! who hereafter shall be criminal,
If precedents are us'd to justify
The blackest crimes.

PUBLIUS
Th' infatuated people
Have called the augurs to the sacred fane,
There to determine this momentous point.

REGULUS
I have no need of oracles, my son;
Honour's the oracle of honest men.
I gave my promise, which I will observe
With most religious strictness. Rome, 'tis true,
Had power to choose the peace, or change of slaves;
But whether Regulus return, or not,
Is his concern, not the concern of Rome.
That was a public, this a private care.
Publius! thy father is not what he was;
I am the slave of Carthage, nor has Rome
Power to dispose of captives not her own.
Guards! let us to the port.—Farewell, my friend.

MANLIUS
Let me entreat thee stay; for shouldst thou go
To stem this tumult of the populace,
They will by force detain thee: then, alas!
Both Regulus and Rome must break their faith.

REGULUS
What! must I then remain?

MANLIUS
No, Regulus,
I will not check thy great career of glory:
Thou shalt depart; meanwhile, I'll try to calm
This wild tumultuous uproar of the people.

The consular authority shall still them.

REGULUS
Thy virtue is my safeguard—but—

MANLIUS
Enough—
I know thy honour, and trust thou to mine.
I am a Roman, and I feel some sparks
Of Regulus's virtue in my breast.
Though fate denies me thy illustrious chains,
I will at least endeavour to deserve them.

[Exit.

REGULUS
How is my country alter'd! how, alas,
Is the great spirit of old Rome extinct!
Restraint and force must now be put to use
To make her virtuous. She must be compell'd
To faith and honour.—Ah! what, Publius here?
And dost thou leave so tamely to my friend
The honour to assist me? Go, my boy,
'Twill make me more in love with chains and death,
To owe them to a son.

PUBLIUS
I go, my father—
I will, I will obey thee.

REGULUS
Do not sigh—
One sigh will check the progress of thy glory.

PUBLIUS
Yes, I will own the pangs of death itself
Would be less cruel than these agonies:
Yet do not frown austerely on thy son:
His anguish is his virtue: if to conquer
The feelings of my soul were easy to me,
'Twould be no merit. Do not then defraud
The sacrifice I make thee of its worth.

[Exeunt severally.

[Enter **ATTILIA.**

ATTILIA (speaking as she enters)

Where is the Consul?—Where, oh, where is Manlius?
I come to breathe the voice of mourning to him,
I come to crave his mercy, to conjure him
To whisper peace to my afflicted bosom,
And heal the anguish of a wounded spirit.

MANLIUS
What would the daughter of my noble friend?

ATTILIA (kneeling)
If ever pity's sweet emotions touch'd thee,—
If ever gentle love assail'd thy breast,—
If ever virtuous friendship fir'd thy soul—
By the dear names of husband and of parent—
By all the soft, yet powerful ties of nature—
If e'er thy lisping infants charm'd thine ear,
And waken'd all the father in thy soul,—
If e'er thou hop'st to have thy latter days
Blest by their love, and sweeten'd by their duty—
Oh, hear a kneeling, weeping, wretched daughter,
Who begs a father's life!—nor hers alone,
But Rome's—his country's father.

MANLIUS
Gentle maid!
Oh, spare this soft, subduing eloquence!—
Nay, rise. I shall forget I am a Roman—
Forget the mighty debt I owe my country—
Forget the fame and glory of thy father.
I must conceal this weakness.

[Turns from her.

ATTILIA (rises eagerly)
Ah! you weep!
Indulge, indulge, my Lord, the virtuous softness:
Was ever sight so graceful, so becoming,
As pity's tear upon the hero's cheek?

MANLIUS
No more—I must not hear thee.

[Going.

ATTILIA
How! not, not hear me!
You must—you shall—nay, nay return, my Lord—
Oh, fly not from me!—look upon my woes,

And imitate the mercy of the gods:
'Tis not their thunder that excites our reverence,
'Tis their mild mercy, and forgiving love.
'Twill add a brighter lustre to thy laurels,
When men shall say, and proudly point thee out,
"Behold the Consul!—He who sav'd his friend."
Oh, what a tide of joy will overwhelm thee!
Who will not envy thee thy glorious feelings?

MANLIUS
Thy father scorns his liberty and life,
Nor will accept of either at the expense
Of honour, virtue, glory, faith, and Rome.

ATTILIA
Think you behold the god-like Regulus
The prey of unrelenting savage foes,
Ingenious only in contriving ill:—
Eager to glut their hunger of revenge,
They'll plot such new, such dire, unheard-of tortures—
Such dreadful, and such complicated vengeance,
As e'en the Punic annals have not known;
And, as they heap fresh torments on his head,
They'll glory in their genius for destruction.
—Ah! Manlius—now methinks I see my father—
My faithful fancy, full of his idea,
Presents him to me—mangled, gash'd, and torn—
Stretch'd on the rack in writhing agony—
The torturing pincers tear his quivering flesh,
While the dire murderers smile upon his wounds,
His groans their music, and his pangs their sport.
And if they lend some interval of ease,
Some dear-bought intermission, meant to make
The following pang more exquisitely felt,
Th' insulting executioners exclaim,
—"Now, Roman! feel the vengeance thou hast scorn'd."

MANLIUS
Repress thy sorrows—

ATTILIA
Can the friend of Regulus
Advise his daughter not to mourn his fate?
How cold, alas! is friendship when compar'd
To ties of blood—to nature's powerful impulse!
Yes—she asserts her empire in my soul,
'Tis Nature pleads—she will—she must be heard;
With warm, resistless eloquence she pleads.—

Ah, thou art soften'd!—see—the Consul yields—
The feelings triumph—tenderness prevails—
The Roman is subdued—the daughter conquers!

[Catching hold of his robe.

MANLIUS
Ah, hold me not!—I must not, cannot stay,
The softness of thy sorrow is contagious;
I, too, may feel when I should only reason.
I dare not hear thee—Regulus and Rome,
The patriot and the friend—all, all forbid it.

[Breaks from her, and exit.

ATTILIA
O feeble grasp!—and is he gone, quite gone?
Hold, hold thy empire, Reason, firmly hold it,
Or rather quit at once thy feeble throne,
Since thou but serv'st to show me what I've lost,
To heighten all the horrors that await me;
To summon up a wild distracted crowd
Of fatal images, to shake my soul,
To scare sweet peace, and banish hope itself.
Farewell! delusive dreams of joy, farewell!
Come, fell Despair! thou pale-ey'd spectre, come,
For thou shalt be Attilia's inmate now,
And thou shalt grow, and twine about her heart,
And she shall be so much enamour'd of thee,
The pageant Pleasure ne'er shall interpose
Her gaudy presence to divide you more.

[Stands in an attitude of silent grief.

[Enter **LICINIUS**.

LICINIUS
At length I've found thee—ah, my charming maid!
How have I sought thee out with anxious fondness!
Alas! she hears me not.—My best Attilia!
Ah! grief oppresses every gentle sense.
Still, still she hears not—'tis Licinius speaks,
He comes to soothe the anguish of thy spirit,
And hush thy tender sorrows into peace.

ATTILIA
Who's he that dares assume the voice of love,
And comes unbidden to these dreary haunts?

Steals on the sacred treasury of woe,
And breaks the league Despair and I have made?

LICINIUS

'Tis one who comes the messenger of heav'n,
To talk of peace, of comfort, and of joy.

ATTILIA

Didst thou not mock me with the sound of joy?
Thou little know'st the anguish of my soul,
If thou believ'st I ever can again,
So long the wretched sport of angry Fortune,
Admit delusive hope to my sad bosom.
No—I abjure the flatterer and her train.
Let those, who ne'er have been like me deceiv'd,
Embrace the fair fantastic sycophant—
For I, alas! am wedded to despair,
And will not hear the sound of comfort more.

LICINIUS

Cease, cease, my love, this tender voice of woe,
Though softer than the dying cygnet's plaint:
She ever chants her most melodious strain
When death and sorrow harmonise her note.

ATTILIA

Yes—I will listen now with fond delight;
For death and sorrow are my darling themes.
Well!—what hast thou to say of death and sorrow?
Believe me, thou wilt find me apt to listen,
And, if my tongue be slow to answer thee,
Instead of words I'll give thee sighs and tears.

LICINIUS

I come to dry thy tears, not make them flow;
The gods once more propitious smile upon us,
Joy shall again await each happy morn,
And ever-new delight shall crown the day!
Yes, Regulus shall live.—

ATTILIA

Ah me! what say'st thou?
Alas! I'm but a poor, weak, trembling woman—
I cannot bear these wild extremes of fate—
Then mock me not.—I think thou art Licinius,
The generous lover, and the faithful friend!
I think thou wouldst not sport with my afflictions.

LICINIUS

Mock thy afflictions?—May eternal Jove,
And every power at whose dread shrine we worship,
Blast all the hopes my fond ideas form,
If I deceive thee! Regulus shall live,
Shall live to give thee to Licinius' arms.
Oh! we will smooth his downward path of life,
And after a long length of virtuous years,
At the last verge of honourable age,
When nature's glimmering lamp goes gently out,
We'll close, together close his eyes in peace—
Together drop the sweetly-painful tear—
Then copy out his virtues in our lives.

ATTILIA

And shall we be so blest? is't possible?
Forgive me, my Licinius, if I doubt thee.
Fate never gave such exquisite delight
As flattering hope hath imag'd to thy soul.
But how?—Explain this bounty of the gods.

LICINIUS

Thou know'st what influence the name of Tribune
Gives its possessor o'er the people's minds:
That power I have exerted, nor in vain;
All are prepar'd to second my designs:
The plot is ripe,—there's not a man but swears
To keep thy god-like father here in Rome—
To save his life at hazard of his own.

ATTILIA

By what gradation does my joy ascend!
I thought that if my father had been sav'd
By any means, I had been rich in bliss:
But that he lives, and lives preserv'd by thee,
Is such a prodigality of fate,
I cannot bear my joy with moderation:
Heav'n should have dealt it with a scantier hand,
And not have shower'd such plenteous blessings on me;
They are too great, too flattering to be real;
'Tis some delightful vision, which enchants,
And cheats my senses, weaken'd by misfortune.

LICINIUS

We'll seek thy father, and meanwhile, my fair,
Compose thy sweet emotions ere thou see'st him,
Pleasure itself is painful in excess;
For joys, like sorrows, in extreme, oppress:

The gods themselves our pious cares approve,
And to reward our virtue crown our love.

ACT V

SCENE - An Apartment in the Ambassador's Palace—Guards and Other Attendants Seen at a Distance

HAMILCAR
Where is this wondrous man, this matchless hero,
This arbiter of kingdoms and of kings,
This delegate of heav'n, this Roman god?
I long to show his soaring mind an equal,
And bring it to the standard of humanity.
What pride, what glory will it be to fix
An obligation on his stubborn soul!
Oh! to constrain a foe to be obliged!
The very thought exalts me e'en to rapture.

[Enter **REGULUS** and **GUARDS**.

HAMILCAR
Well, Regulus!—At last—

REGULUS
I know it all;
I know the motive of thy just complaint—
Be not alarm'd at this licentious uproar
Of the mad populace. I will depart—
Fear not—I will not stay in Rome alive.

HAMILCAR
What dost thou mean by uproar and alarms?
Hamilcar does not come to vent complaints;
He rather comes to prove that Afric, too,
Produces heroes, and that Tiber's banks
May find a rival on the Punic coast.

REGULUS
Be it so.—'Tis not a time for vain debate:
Collect thy people.—Let us strait depart.

HAMILCAR
Lend me thy hearing, first.

REGULUS
O patience, patience!

HAMILCAR
Is it esteem'd a glory to be grateful?

REGULUS
The time has been when 'twas a duty only,
But 'tis a duty now so little practis'd,
That to perform it is become a glory.

HAMILCAR
If to fulfil it should expose to danger?—

REGULUS
It rises then to an illustrious virtue.

HAMILCAR
Then grant this merit to an African.
Give me a patient hearing—Thy great son,
As delicate in honour as in love,
Hath nobly given my Barce to my arms;
And yet I know he doats upon the maid.
I come to emulate the generous deed;
He gave me back my love, and in return
I will restore his father.

REGULUS
Ah! what say'st thou?
Wilt thou preserve me then?

HAMILCAR
I will.

REGULUS
But how?

HAMILCAR
By leaving thee at liberty to fly.

REGULUS
Ah!

HAMILCAR
I will dismiss my guards on some pretence,
Meanwhile do thou escape, and lie conceal'd:
I will affect a rage I shall not feel,
Unmoor my ships, and sail for Africa.

REGULUS

Abhorr'd barbarian!

HAMILCAR
Well, what dost thou say?
Art thou not much surpris'd?

REGULUS
I am, indeed.

HAMILCAR
Thou could'st not then have hop'd it?

REGULUS
No! I could not.

HAMILCAR
And yet I'm not a Roman.

REGULUS (smiling contemptuously)
I perceive it.

HAMILCAR (aloud to the **GUARDS**)
You may retire

REGULUS
No!—Stay, I charge you stay.

HAMILCAR
And wherefore stay?

REGULUS
I thank thee for thy offer,
But I shall go with thee.

HAMILCAR
'Tis well, proud man!
Thou dost despise me, then?

REGULUS
No—but I pity thee.

HAMILCAR
Why pity me?

REGULUS
Because thy poor dark soul
Hath never felt the piercing ray of virtue.
Know, African! the scheme thou dost propose

Would injure me, thy country, and thyself.

HAMILCAR
Thou dost mistake.

REGULUS
Who was it gave thee power
To rule the destiny of Regulus?
Am I a slave to Carthage, or to thee?

HAMILCAR
What does it signify from whom, proud Roman!
Thou dost receive this benefit?

REGULUS
A benefit?
O savage ignorance! is it a benefit
To lie, elope, deceive, and be a villain?

HAMILCAR
What! not when life itself, when all's at stake?
Know'st thou my countrymen prepare thee tortures
That shock imagination but to think of?
Thou wilt be mangled, butcher'd, rack'd, impal'd.
Does not thy nature shrink?

REGULUS (smiling at his threats)
Hamilcar! no.
Dost thou not know the Roman genius better?
We live on honour—'tis our food, our life.
The motive, and the measure of our deeds!
We look on death as on a common object;
The tongue nor faulters, nor the cheek turns pale,
Nor the calm eye is mov'd at sight of him:
We court, and we embrace him undismay'd;
We smile at tortures if they lead to glory,
And only cowardice and guilt appal us.

HAMILCAR
Fine sophistry! the valour of the tongue,
The heart disclaims it; leave this pomp of words,
And cease dissembling with a friend like me.
I know that life is dear to all who live,
That death is dreadful,—yes, and must be fear'd,
E'en by the frozen apathists of Rome.

REGULUS
Did I fear death when on Bagrada's banks

I fac'd and slew the formidable serpent
That made your boldest Africans recoil,
And shrink with horror, though the monster liv'd
A native inmate of their own parch'd deserts?
Did I fear death before the gates of Adis?—
Ask Bostar, or let Asdrubal confess.

HAMILCAR
Or shall I rather of Xantippus ask,
Who dar'd to undeceive deluded Rome,
And prove this vaunter not invincible?
'Tis even said, in Africa I mean,
He made a prisoner of this demigod.—
Did we not triumph then?

REGULUS
Vain boaster! no.
No Carthaginian conquer'd Regulus;
Xantippus was a Greek—a brave one too:
Yet what distinction did your Afric make
Between the man who serv'd her, and her foe:
I was the object of her open hate;
He, of her secret, dark malignity.
He durst not trust the nation he had sav'd;
He knew, and therefore fear'd you.—Yes, he knew
Where once you were oblig'd you ne'er forgave.
Could you forgive at all, you'd rather pardon
The man who hated, than the man who serv'd you.
Xantippus found his ruin ere it reach'd him,
Lurking behind your honours and rewards;
Found it in your feign'd courtesies and fawnings.
When vice intends to strike a master stroke,
Its veil is smiles, its language protestations.
The Spartan's merit threaten'd, but his service
Compell'd his ruin.—Both you could not pardon.

HAMILCAR
Come, come, I know full well—

REGULUS
Barbarian! peace.
I've heard too much.—Go, call thy followers:
Prepare thy ships, and learn to do thy duty.

HAMILCAR
Yes!—show thyself intrepid, and insult me;
Call mine the blindness of barbarian friendship.
On Tiber's banks I hear thee, and am calm:

But know, thou scornful Roman! that too soon
In Carthage thou may'st fear and feel my vengeance:
Thy cold, obdurate pride shall there confess,
Though Rome may talk—'tis Africa can punish.

[Exit.

REGULUS
Farewell! I've not a thought to waste on thee.
Where is the Consul? why does Publius stay?
Alas! I fear—but see Attilia comes!—

[Enter **ATTILIA**.

REGULUS
What brings thee here, my child? what eager joy
Transports thee thus?

ATTILIA
I cannot speak—my father!
Joy chokes my utterance—Rome, dear grateful Rome,
(Oh, may her cup with blessings overflow!)
Gives up our common destiny to thee;
Faithful and constant to th' advice thou gav'st her,
She will not hear of peace, or change of slaves,
But she insists—reward and bless her, gods!—
That thou shalt here remain.

REGULUS
What! with the shame—

ATTILIA
Oh! no—the sacred senate hath consider'd
That when to Carthage thou did'st pledge thy faith,
Thou wast a captive, and that being such,
Thou could'st not bind thyself in covenant.

REGULUS
He who can die, is always free, my child!
Learn farther, he who owns another's strength
Confesses his own weakness.—Let them know,
I swore I would return because I chose it,
And will return, because I swore to do it.

[Enter **PUBLIUS**.

PUBLIUS
Vain is that hope, my father.

REGULUS
Who shall stop me?

PUBLIUS
All Rome.—The citizens are up in arms:
In vain would reason stop the growing torrent;
In vain wouldst thou attempt to reach the port,
The way is barr'd by thronging multitudes:
The other streets of Rome are all deserted.

REGULUS
Where, where is Manlius?

PUBLIUS
He is still thy friend:
His single voice opposes a whole people;
He threats this moment and the next entreats,
But all in vain; none hear him, none obey.
The general fury rises e'en to madness.
The axes tremble in the lictors' hands,
Who, pale and spiritless, want power to use them—
And one wild scene of anarchy prevails.

REGULUS
Farewell! my daughter. Publius, follow me.

[Exit **PUBLIUS**.

ATTILIA
Ah! where? I tremble—

[Detaining **REGULUS**.

REGULUS
To assist my friend—
T' upbraid my hapless country with her crime—
To keep unstain'd the glory of these chains—
To go, or perish.

ATTILIA
Oh! have mercy!

REGULUS
Hold;
I have been patient with thee; have indulg'd
Too much the fond affections of thy soul;
It is enough; thy grief would now offend

Thy father's honour; do not let thy tears
Conspire with Rome to rob me of my triumph.

ATTILIA
Alas! it wounds my soul.

REGULUS
I know it does.
I know 'twill grieve thy gentle heart to lose me;
But think, thou mak'st the sacrifice to Rome,
And all is well again.

ATTILIA
Alas! my father,
In aught beside—

REGULUS
What wouldst thou do, my child?
Canst thou direct the destiny of Rome,
And boldly plead amid the assembled senate?
Canst thou, forgetting all thy sex's softness,
Fiercely engage in hardy deeds of arms?
Canst thou encounter labour, toil and famine,
Fatigue and hardships, watchings, cold and heat?
Canst thou attempt to serve thy country thus?
Thou canst not:—but thou may'st sustain my loss
Without these agonising pains of grief,
And set a bright example of submission,
Worthy a Roman's daughter.

ATTILIA
Yet such fortitude—

REGULUS
Is a most painful virtue;—but Attilia
Is Regulus's daughter, and must have it.

ATTILIA
I will entreat the gods to give it me.
Ah! thou art offended! I have lost thy love.

REGULUS
Is this concern a mark that thou hast lost it?
I cannot, cannot spurn my weeping child.
Receive this proof of my paternal fondness;—
Thou lov'st Licinius—he too loves my daughter.
I give thee to his wishes; I do more—
I give thee to his virtues.—Yes, Attilia,

The noble youth deserves this dearest pledge
Thy father's friendship ever can bestow.

ATTILIA
My lord! my father! wilt thou, canst thou leave me?
The tender father will not quit his child!

REGULUS
I am, I am thy father! as a proof,
I leave thee my example how to suffer.
My child! I have a heart within this bosom;
That heart has passions—see in what we differ;
Passion—which is thy tyrant—is my slave.

ATTILIA
Ah! stay my father. Ah!—

REGULUS
Farewell! farewell!

[Exit.

ATTILIA
Yes, Regulus! I feel thy spirit here,
Thy mighty spirit struggling in this breast,
And it shall conquer all these coward feelings,
It shall subdue the woman in my soul;
A Roman virgin should be something more—
Should dare above her sex's narrow limits—
And I will dare—and mis'ry shall assist me—
My father! I will be indeed thy daughter!
The hero shall no more disdain his child;
Attilia shall not be the only branch
That yields dishonour to the parent tree.

[Enter **BARCE**.

BARCE
Attilia! is it true that Regulus,
In spite of senate, people, augurs, friends,
And children, will depart?

ATTILIA
Yes, it is true.

BARCE
Oh! what romantic madness!

ATTILIA
You forget—
Barce! the deeds of heroes claim respect.

BARCE
Dost thou approve a virtue which must lead
To chains, to tortures, and to certain death?

ATTILIA
Barce! those chains, those tortures, and that death,
Will be his triumph.

BARCE
Thou art pleas'd, Attilia:
By heav'n thou dost exult in his destruction!

ATTILIA
Ah! pitying powers.

[Weeps.

BARCE
I do not comprehend thee.

ATTILIA
No, Barce, I believe it.—Why, how shouldst thou?
If I mistake not, thou wast born in Carthage,
In a barbarian land, where never child
Was taught to triumph in a father's chains.

BARCE
Yet thou dost weep—thy tears at least are honest,
For they refuse to share thy tongue's deceit;
They speak the genuine language of affliction,
And tell the sorrows that oppress thy soul.

ATTILIA
Grief, that dissolves in tears, relieves the heart.
When congregated vapours melt in rain,
The sky is calm'd, and all's serene again.

[Exit.

BARCE
Why, what a strange, fantastic land is this!
This love of glory's the disease of Rome;
It makes her mad, it is a wild delirium,
An universal and contagious frenzy;

It preys on all, it spares nor sex nor age:
The Consul envies Regulus his chains—
He, not less mad, contemns his life and freedom—
The daughter glories in the father's ruin—
And Publius, more distracted than the rest,
Resigns the object that his soul adores,
For this vain phantom, for this empty glory.
This may be virtue; but I thank the gods,
The soul of Barce's not a Roman soul.

[Exit.

SCENE—Within Sight of the Tiber

Ships ready for the embarkation of **REGULUS** and the **AMBASSADOR—TRIBUNE** and **PEOPLE** stopping up the passage—**CONSUL** and **LICTORS** endeavouring to clear it.

MANLIUS and **LICINIUS** advance.

LICINIUS
Rome will not suffer Regulus to go.

MANLIUS
I thought the Consul and the Senators
Had been a part of Rome.

LICINIUS
I grant they are—
But still the people are the greater part.

MANLIUS
The greater, not the wiser.

LICINIUS
The less cruel.—
Full of esteem and gratitude to Regulus,
We would preserve his life.

MANLIUS
And we his honour.

LICINIUS
His honour!—

MANLIUS
Yes. Time presses. Words are vain.

Make way there—clear the passage.

LICINIUS
On your lives,
Stir not a man.

MANLIUS
I do command you, go.

LICINIUS
And I forbid it.

MANLIUS
Clear the way, my friends.
How dares Licinius thus oppose the Consul?

LICINIUS
How dar'st thou, Manlius, thus oppose the Tribune?

MANLIUS
I'll show thee what I dare, imprudent boy!—
Lictors, force through the passage.

LICINIUS
Romans, guard it.

MANLIUS
Gods! is my power resisted then with arms?
Thou dost affront the Majesty of Rome.

LICINIUS
The Majesty of Rome is in the people;
Thou dost insult it by opposing them.

PEOPLE
Let noble Regulus remain in Rome.

MANLIUS
My friends, let me explain this treacherous scheme.

PEOPLE
We will not hear thee—Regulus shall stay.

MANLIUS
What! none obey me?

PEOPLE
Regulus shall stay.

MANLIUS Romans, attend.—

PEOPLE
Let Regulus remain.

[Enter **REGULUS**, followed by **PUBLIUS, ATTILIA, HAMILCAR, BARCE**, &c.

REGULUS
Let Regulus remain! What do I hear?
Is't possible the wish should come from you?
Can Romans give, or Regulus accept,
A life of infamy? Is't possible?
Where is the ancient virtue of my country?
Rise, rise, ye mighty spirits of old Rome!
I do invoke you from your silent tombs;
Fabricius, Cocles, and Camillus, rise,
And show your sons what their great fathers were.
My countrymen, what crime have I committed?
Alas! how has the wretched Regulus
Deserv'd your hatred?

LICINIUS
Hatred? ah! my friend,
It is our love would break these cruel chains.

REGULUS
If you deprive me of my chains, I'm nothing;
They are my honours, riches, titles,—all!
They'll shame my enemies, and grace my country;
They'll waft her glory to remotest climes,
Beyond her provinces and conquer'd realms,
Where yet her conq'ring eagles never flew;
Nor shall she blush hereafter if she find
Recorded with her faithful citizens
The name of Regulus, the captive Regulus.
My countrymen! what, think you, kept in awe
The Volsci, Sabines, Æqui, and Hernici?
The arms of Rome alone? no, 'twas her virtue;
That sole surviving good, which brave men keep
Though fate and warring worlds combine against them:
This still is mine—and I'll preserve it, Romans!
The wealth of Plutus shall not bribe it from me!
If you, alas! require this sacrifice,
Carthage herself was less my foe than Rome;
She took my freedom—she could take no more;
But Rome, to crown her work, would take my honour.
My friends! if you deprive me of my chains,

I am no more than any other slave:
Yes, Regulus becomes a common captive,
A wretched, lying, perjur'd fugitive!
But if, to grace my bonds, you leave my honour,
I shall be still a Roman, though a slave.

LICINIUS
What faith should be observ'd with savages?
What promise should be kept which bonds extort?

REGULUS
Unworthy subterfuge! ah! let us leave
To the wild Arab and the faithless Moor
These wretched maxims of deceit and fraud:
Examples ne'er can justify the coward:
The brave man never seeks a vindication,
Save from his own just bosom and the gods;
From principle, not precedent, he acts:
As that arraigns him, or as that acquits,
He stands or falls; condemn'd or justified.

LICINIUS
Rome is no more if Regulus departs.

REGULUS
Let Rome remember Regulus must die!
Nor would the moment of my death be distant,
If nature's work had been reserv'd for nature:
What Carthage means to do, she would have done
As speedily, perhaps, at least as surely.
My wearied life has almost reach'd its goal;
The once-warm current stagnates in these veins,
Or through its icy channels slowly creeps—
View the weak arm; mark the pale furrow'd cheek,
The slacken'd sinew, and the dim sunk eye,
And tell me then I must not think of dying!
How can I serve you else? My feeble limbs
Would totter now beneath the armour's weight,
The burden of that body it once shielded.
You see, my friends, you see, my countrymen,
I can no longer show myself a Roman,
Except by dying like one.—Gracious Heaven
Points out a way to crown my days with glory;
Oh, do not frustrate, then, the will of Jove,
And close a life of virtue with disgrace!
Come, come, I know my noble Romans better;
I see your souls, I read repentance in them;
You all applaud me—nay, you wish my chains:

'Twas nothing but excess of love misled you,
And as you're Romans you will conquer that.
Yes!—I perceive your weakness is subdu'd—
Seize, seize the moment of returning virtue;
Throw to the ground, my sons, those hostile arms;
Retard no longer Regulus's triumph;
I do request it of you, as a friend,
I call you to your duty, as a patriot,
And—were I still your gen'ral, I'd command you.

LICINIUS [To the **PEOPLE**, who clear the way, and quit their arms.
Lay down your arms—let Regulus depart.

REGULUS
Gods! gods! I thank you—you indeed are righteous.

PUBLIUS
See every man disarm'd. Oh, Rome! oh, father!

ATTILIA
Hold, hold my heart. Alas! they all obey.

REGULUS
The way is clear. Hamilcar, I attend thee.

HAMILCAR
Why, I begin to envy this old man! [Aside.

MANLIUS
Not the proud victor on the day of triumph,
Warm from the slaughter of dispeopled realms,
Though conquer'd princes grace his chariot wheels,
Though tributary monarchs wait his nod,
And vanquish'd nations bend the knee before him,
E'er shone with half the lustre that surrounds
This voluntary sacrifice for Rome!
Who loves his country will obey her laws;
Who most obeys them is the truest patriot.

REGULUS
Be our last parting worthy of ourselves.
Farewell! my friends.—I bless the gods who rule us,
Since I must leave you, that I leave you Romans.
Preserve the glorious name untainted still,
And you shall be the rulers of the globe,
The arbiters of earth. The farthest east,
Beyond where Ganges rolls his rapid flood,
Shall proudly emulate the Roman name.

(Kneels)

Ye gods, the guardians of this glorious people,
Who watch with jealous eye Æneas' race,
This land of heroes I commit to you!
This ground, these walls, this people be your care!
Oh! bless them, bless them with a liberal hand!
Let fortitude and valour, truth and justice,
For ever flourish and increase among them!
And if some baneful planet threat the Capitol
With its malignant influence, oh, avert it!—
Be Regulus the victim of your wrath.—
On this white head be all your vengeance pour'd,
But spare, oh, spare, and bless immortal Rome!
Ah! tears? my Romans weep? Farewell! farewell!

[ATTILIA struggles to get to REGULUS—is prevented—she faints—he fixes his eye steadily on her for some time, and then departs to the ships.

MANLIUS (looking after him)
Farewell! farewell! thou glory of mankind!
Protector, father, saviour of thy country!
Through Regulus the Roman name shall live,
Shall triumph over time, and mock oblivion.
Farewell! thou pride of this immortal coast!
'Tis Rome alone a Regulus can boast.

EPILOGUE

What son of physic, but his art extends,
As well as hand, when call'd on by his friends?
What landlord is so weak to make you fast,
When guests like you bespeak a good repast?
But weaker still were he whom fate has plac'd
To soothe your cares, and gratify your taste,
Should he neglect to bring before your eyes
Those dainty dramas which from genius rise;
Whether your luxury be to smile or weep,
His and your profits just proportion keep.
To-night he brought, nor fears a due reward,
A Roman Patriot by a Female Bard.
Britons who feel his flame, his worth will rate,
No common spirit his, no common fate.
INFLEXIBLE and CAPTIVE must be great.
"How!" cries a sucking fop, thus lounging, straddling

(Whose head shows want of ballast by its nodding),
"A woman write? Learn, Madam, of your betters,
And read a noble Lord's Post-hù-mous Letters.
There you will learn the sex may merit praise
By making puddings—not by making plays:
They can make tea and mischief, dance and sing;
Their heads, though full of feathers, can't take wing."
I thought they could, Sir; now and then by chance,
Maids fly to Scotland, and some wives to France.
He still went nodding on—"Do all she can,
Woman's a trifle—play-thing—like her fan."
Right, Sir, and when a wife the rattle of a man.
And shall such things as these become the test
Of female worth? the fairest and the best
Of all heaven's creatures? for so Milton sung us,
And, with such champions, who shall dare to wrong us?
Come forth, proud man, in all your pow'rs array'd;
Shine out in all your splendour—Who's afraid?
Who on French wit has made a glorious war,
Defended Shakspeare, and subdu'd Voltaire?—

1ˢᵗ WOMAN
—Who, rich in knowledge, knows no pride,
Can boast ten tongues, and yet not satisfied?

2ⁿᵈ WOMAN
—Who lately sung the sweetest lay?
A woman! woman! woman! still I say.
Well, then, who dares deny our power and might?
Will any married man dispute our right?
Speak boldly, Sirs,—your wives are not in sight.
What! are you silent? then you are content;
Silence, the proverb tells us, gives consent.
Critics, will you allow our honest claim?
Are you dumb, too? This night has fix'd our fame.

Hannah More - A Short Biography

Hannah More was born on February 2ⁿᵈ, 1745 at Fishponds in the parish of Stapleton, near Bristol. She was the fourth of five daughters of Jacob More, a schoolmaster. He was originally from a family of Presbyterians in Norfolk, but had become a member of the Church of England to pursue a career in the Church. After losing a lawsuit over an estate he had hoped to inherit, he moved to Bristol, becoming an excise officer and later a teacher at the Fishponds free school.

The City of Bristol, at that time, was a centre for slave-trading and Hannah would, over time, become one of its staunchest critics.

The More's were a close family and all the sisters were educated at first by their father who taught them Latin and mathematics. Hannah was also taught French by her elder sisters. Her conversational French was improved by time spent with French prisoners of war from the Seven-Year's-War in Frenchay, then a small village near Bristol.

She was keen to learn, possessed a sharp intellect and was assiduous in studying and, according to family tradition, began writing at an early age.

In 1758 Jacob established his own girls' boarding school at Trinity Street in Bristol for the elder sisters, Mary and Elizabeth, to run. Hannah became a pupil there when she was 12. Jacob and his wife moved to Stony Hill in the city to open a school for boys.

Hannah became a teacher at her sister's school and it was here that she produced her first literary efforts. These were prompted by trying to find material suitable for her young charges to act in. Her first, written in 1762, was The Search after Happiness (by the mid-1780s some 10,000 copies had been sold).

In 1767 Hannah gave up her share in the school to become engaged to William Turner. After six years, with no wedding in sight, and Turner reluctant to move forward, the engagement was broken off. It was now 1773 and by all accounts Hannah suffered a nervous breakdown and spent some time recuperating in nearby Uphill. Turner then bestowed upon her an annual annuity of £200. This was enough to meet her needs and set her free to pursue a literary career. With that ambition London was her next stop. She travelled there in the winter of 1773/74 together with her sisters, Sarah and Martha.

She had previously written some verses on a production of King Lear staged by the famous actor David Garrick and this led to a lasting friendship with him and a pivotal introduction to the London Literary society. Now she met and charmed Samuel Johnson, Joshua Reynolds and Edmund Burke. Johnson is quoted as saying to her "Madam, before you flatter a man so grossly to his face, you should consider whether or not your flattery is worth having." He would later be quoted as calling her "the finest versifatrix in the English language".

Hannah also became a leading member of the Bluestocking group of women who met to further literary and intellectual pursuits. Here she met women who were to become life-long friends; Elizabeth Montagu, Frances Boscawen, Elizabeth Carter, Elizabeth Vesey and Hester Chapone (Hannah later wrote a celebration of this circle in her 1782 poem The Bas Bleu, or, Conversation, published in 1784).

Her first play, The Inflexible Captive, was staged at Bath in 1775. It was based on the opera, Attilio Regulo, by the Italian Pietro Metastasio (1698-1782) whose works she admired.

Her theatrical career was now in full swing. David Garrick himself produced her next play, Percy, in 1777 as well as writing both the Prologue and Epilogue for it. It was a great success when performed at Covent Garden in December of that year. Her next play, Fatal Falsehood, was staged in 1779, shortly after the death of Garrick. It was less successful but still admired.

With David Garrick now passed (January 20th, 1779) Hannah came to view the theatre as both morally wrong and not where her ambitions now lay. She now began to spend her time advancing her interests in other areas.

In 1781 she first met Horace Walpole, man of letters art historian and Whig politician and now corresponded regularly with him.

A friendship with James Oglethorpe, who had long been concerned with slavery as a moral issue and who was working with Granville Sharp in an early abolitionist capacity, started to awaken Hannah's social conscious.

Hannah turned to religious writing, beginning with her Sacred Dramas in 1782; it rapidly ran through nineteen editions. These and the poems Bas-Bleu and Florio (1786) mark her gradual transition to a more serious and considered view of life and are fully expressed in her Thoughts on the Importance of the Manners of the Great to General Society (1788), and An Estimate of the Religion of the Fashionable World (1790).

In Bristol, in 1784, she discovered the poet Ann Yearsley, the so-called 'poetical milkmaid of Bristol'. With Yearsley destitute, Hannah raised a considerable sum of money for her. Lactilia, as Yearsley was known, published Poems, on Several Occasions in 1785, earning about £600. Hannah and Elizabeth Montagu held the profits in trust to protect them from Yearsley's husband. However Ann wished for the capital to be made over, and made insinuations of stealing against Hannah. The money was released and Hannah felt her reputation had been tarnished.

With the death of Samuel Johnson in December 1784, Hannah moved, with her sister Martha, in 1795, to a cottage at Cowslip Green, near Wrington in rural Somerset, "to escape from the world gradually".

In the summer of 1786, she spent time with Sir Charles and Lady Margaret Middleton at their home in Teston in Kent. Among their guests was the local vicar James Ramsay and a young Thomas Clarkson, both of whom were central to the early abolition campaign against slavery.

In 1787, she met John Newton and the 'Clapham Sect' (a group of wealthy evangelical Christians who lived near Clapham and met at Henry Thornton's house). The group was strongly opposed to the Slave Trade. William Wilberforce was a member of the group and he and Hannah became firm friends.

Hannah contributed much to the running of the newly-founded Abolition Society including, in February 1788, her publication of Slavery, a Poem which has long been recognised as one of the most important poems of the abolition period. The poem dramatically described a mistreated, enslaved female separated from her children and severely questioned Britain's role in the Slave Trade.

Her relationship with members of the society, especially Wilberforce, was close. She spent the summer of 1789 holidaying with Wilberforce in the Peak District, planning for the abolition campaign, which, at the time, was at its height.

Her work now became more evangelical. In the 1790s she wrote several Cheap Repository Tracts which covered moral, religious and political topics and were both for sale or distributed to literate poor people. This coincided with her increasing philanthropic work in the Mendip area.

Beyond any doubt, Hannah was the most influential female member of the Society for Effecting the Abolition of the African Slave Trade.

Hannah wrote many ethical books and tracts: Strictures on the Modern System of Female Education (1799), Hints towards Forming the Character of a Young Princess (1805), Cœlebs in Search of a Wife (only nominally a story, 1809), Practical Piety (1811), Christian Morals (1813), Character of St Paul (1815), Moral Sketches (1819). She was a rapid writer, and her work is consequently discursive, animated and without a rigorous structure.

However the originality and force of Hannah's writings perhaps explains her extraordinary popularity. At the behest of Beilby Porteus, Bishop of London and a leading abolitionist, Hannah wrote many spirited rhymes and prose tales, the earliest of which was Village Politics, by Will Chip (1792), intended to counteract the doctrines of Thomas Paine and the influence of the French Revolution.

The series of Cheap Repository Tracts, eventually led to the formation of the Religious Tracts Society. The Tracts were produced at the rate of three a month between 1795 and 1797.

The most famous is perhaps The Shepherd of Salisbury Plain, describing a family of incredible frugality and contentment. Two million copies of these rapid and telling sketches were circulated, in one year, teaching the poor in rhetoric of the most ingenious homeliness to rely upon the virtues of content, sobriety, humility, industry and reverence for the British Constitution, hatred of the French, trust in God and in the kindness of the gentry.

Several of the Tracts oppose slavery and the slave trade, in particular, the poem The Sorrows of Yamba; or, The Negro Woman's Lamentation, which appeared in November 1795 and which was co-authored with Eaglesfield Smith. However, the tracts have also been noted for their encouragement of social quietism in an age of revolution.

In 1789, she purchased a small house at Cowslip Green in Somerset. Wilberforce encouraged Hannah to set up a Sunday school in Cheddar, where poor children could be taught to read. Soon she and her sisters had set up similar schools throughout the Mendip villages, despite fierce opposition.

She was instrumental in setting up twelve schools by 1800 where reading, the Bible and the catechism were taught to local children. Hannah also donated money to Bishop Philander Chase for the founding of Kenyon College, and a portrait of her hangs there in Peirce Hall.

John Scandrett Harford of Blaise Castle was a prodigious benefactor to More's schools in the 1790s, and Hannah modeled the idealised hero and heroine in Cœlebs in Search of Wife (1809) on Mr and Mrs Harford.

However it cannot be said that Hannah was a staunch supporter of Women's rights. She refused to read Mary Wollstonecraft's Rights of Women, saying "so many women are fond of government... because they are not fit for it. To be unstable and capricious is but too characteristic of our sex". She was also shocked by the movement for female education in France, saying "they run to study philosophy, and neglect their families to be present at lectures in anatomy". She is also said to have turned down an honorary membership of the Royal Society of Literature because she considered her "sex alone a disqualification".

The More sisters also met with a good deal of opposition in their philanthropic works: the farmers thought that education, even to the limited extent of learning to read, would be fatal to agriculture, and the clergy, whose neglect she was making good, accused her of Methodist tendencies.

She continued to oppose slavery throughout her life, but at the time of the Abolition Bill of 1807 (which outlawed the slave trade, but not slavery itself), her health did not permit her to take as active a role in the movement as she had done in the late 1780s, although she maintained a correspondence with Wilberforce and others Abolitionists.

In her later life, she continued to dedicate much of her time to religious writing. Nevertheless, her most popular work was a novel, Cœlebs in Search of a Wife, which appeared in two volumes in 1809 (and which ran to nine editions in 1809 alone).

In 1816, Hannah was still at odds with the French. Following Waterloo she is quoted as saying that 'peace with France is a worse evil than war', and refused to allow a French translation of Cœlebs.

Her last few years were spent at Clifton, people from all parts came to visit her even though her health was fading and she was writing less often.

She lived just long enough to see the act finally abolishing slavery. In July 1833, the Bill to abolish slavery throughout the British Empire passed in the House of Commons, followed by the House of Lords on August 1st.

Hannah More died on September 7th, 1833. She is buried at Church of All Saints, Wrington. In her will she left more than £30,000 to charities and religious societies, the equivalent today of many millions.

www.ingramcontent.com/pod-product-compliance
Lightning Source LLC
Chambersburg PA
CBHW060146050426

42448CB00010B/2323